Grade 8 · Unit 3

California Inspire Science

Understanding Waves

Mc
Graw
Hill

Phenomenon: Light Waves

Drops of dew on a flower stem show miniature images of the large daisy in the background. The image of the spoon in a glass of water shows additional effects of light waves and how we perceive them.

Fun Fact

Light typically travels in a straight line but may be bent when passing through different substances.

FRONT COVER: (t)Horst Bierau Photography - foto.bierau.net/Moment/Getty Images, (b)azwanlazam/Shutterstock. **BACK COVER:** Horst Bierau Photography - foto.bierau.net/Moment/Getty Images.

mheducation.com/prek-12

Copyright © 2020 McGraw-Hill Education

Send all inquiries to:
McGraw-Hill Education
STEM Learning Solutions Center
8787 Orion Place
Columbus, OH 43240

ISBN: 978-0-07-684112-7
MHID: 0-07-684112-X

Printed in the United States of America.

5 6 7 8 9 LMN 23 22 21 20

McGraw-Hill is committed to providing instructional materials in Science, Technology, Engineering, and Mathematics (STEM) that give all students a solid foundation, one that prepares them for college and careers in the 21st century.

Welcome to

California Inspire Science

Explore Our Phenomenal World

Learning begins with curiosity. Inspire Science is designed to spark your interest and empower you to ask more questions, think more critically, and generate innovative ideas.

Start exploring now!

Inspire Curiosity • Inspire Investigation • Inspire Innovation

i

Program Authors

Alton L. Biggs
Biggs Educational Consulting
Commerce, TX

Ralph M. Feather, Jr., PhD
Professor of Educational Studies and
Secondary Education
Bloomsburg University
Bloomsburg, PA

Douglas Fisher, PhD
Professor of Teacher Education
San Diego State University
San Diego, CA

Page Keeley, MEd
Author, Consultant, Inventor of
Page Keeley Science Probes
Maine Mathematics and Science
Alliance
Augusta, ME

Michael Manga, PhD
Professor
University of California, Berkeley
Berkeley, CA

Edward P. Ortleb
Science/Safety Consultant
St. Louis, MO

Dinah Zike, MEd
Author, Consultant, Inventor
of Foldables®
Dinah Zike Academy, Dinah-Might
Adventures, LP
San Antonio, TX

Advisors

Phil Lafontaine
NGSS Education Consultant
Folsom, CA

Donna Markey
NBCT, Vista Unified School District
Vista, CA

Julie Olson
NGSS Consultant
Mitchell Senior High/Second Chance
High School
Mitchell, SD

California Teacher Advisory Board

Summer Agnes
Rosemead SD
Rosemead, CA

Nancy Cotter
San Marcos USD
San Marcos, CA

Bonnie Neally
Long Beach USD
Long Beach, CA

Diane Newell
Los Angeles USD
Los Angeles, CA

Ray Pietersen
Elk Grove USD
Elk Grove, CA

Rosie Vanzyl
Los Angeles USD
Los Angeles, CA

Joyce Wilkinson
Salinas Union SD
Salinas, CA

Content Consultants

Chris Anderson
STEM Coach and Engineering
Consultant
Cinnaminson, NJ

Emily Miller
EL Consultant
Madison, WI

Key Partners

American Museum of Natural History

The American Museum of Natural History is one of the world's preeminent scientific and cultural institutions. Founded in 1869, the Museum has advanced its global mission to discover, interpret, and disseminate information about human cultures, the natural world, and the universe through a wide-ranging program of scientific research, education, and exhibition.

PhET Interactive Simulations

The PhET Interactive Simulations project at the University of Colorado Boulder provides teachers and students with interactive science and math simulations. Based on extensive education research, PhET simulations engage students through an intuitive, game-like environment where students learn through exploration and discovery.

SpongeLab Interactives

SpongeLab Interactives is a learning technology company that inspires learning and engagement by creating gamified environments that encourage students to interact with digital learning experiences. Students participate in inquiry activities and problem-solving to explore a variety of topics through the use of games, interactives, and video while teachers take advantage of formative, summative, or performance-based assessment information that is gathered through the learning management system.

AdvancED | Measured Progress, a nonprofit organization, is a pioneer in authentic, standards-based assessments with a focus on data-driven tools for improvement. Teachers and students are provided with meaningful assessment that includes robust performance tasks. The assessment content enables teachers to monitor student progress toward learning NGSS.

PhET Interactive Simulations/University of Colorado Boulder/https://phet.colorado.edu

Table of Contents
Understanding Waves

Introduction to Waves

 Zuma Beach in Malibu, CA

ENCOUNTER
THE PHENOMENON

Why does a wave knock you down?

[Catch a Wave]

GO ONLINE
Watch the video *Catch a Wave* to see this phenomenon in action.

Communicate Think about why waves knock you down. Record your ideas for how or why you think this happens below. Discuss your ideas with three different partners. Revise or update your ideas, if necessary, after the discussions with your classmates.

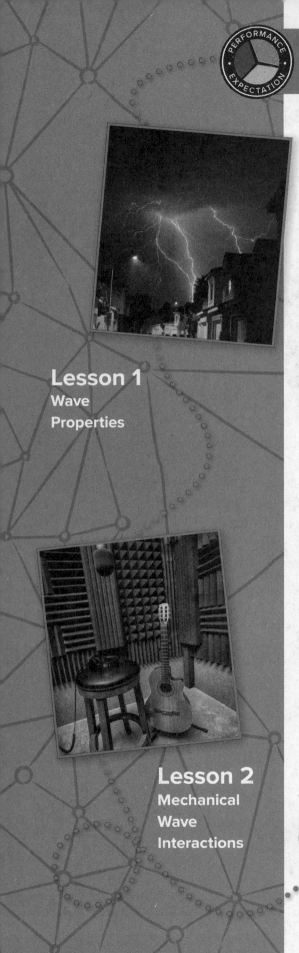
Don't Make Waves

During the Atlantic hurricane season, videos of huge waves crashing against the shore are commonly seen on national weather reports. These waves are known to cause extensive beach damage to shorelines. Many coastal areas are known for their beaches, which are major tourism draws to their communities.

One coastal community is looking to install a preventive measure to reduce the damage to the beach caused by waves during storms. You have been selected to be a part of a committee that will evaluate different preventive designs. You will choose which design will be the most economical for your community and build a model to demonstrate how the design will help protect the beach.

Start Thinking About It

Recall a time when you made waves. How did you make them? Were you able to change the wave? Discuss your thoughts with your partner.

Lesson 1
Wave Properties

Lesson 2
Mechanical Wave Interactions

STEM Module Project
Planning and Completing the Engineering Challenge

How will you meet this goal? The concepts you will learn throughout this module will help you plan and complete the Engineering Challenge. Just follow the prompts at the end of each lesson!

Getting the Ball Back

Two brothers are playing soccer on the beach. One brother kicks the ball really hard and the ball lands in the water, about 50 meters from the beach. They wonder if the ball will float back to the beach. This is what they said:

Todd: Waves carry objects as they travel through water. If we wait, the waves will move the ball back onto the beach.

Brian: Waves don't carry things as they travel through water. I think we need to swim out and get the ball.

Who do you agree with?_____ Explain why you agree using ideas about waves.

_____

_____

_____

_____

_____

You will revisit your response to the Science Probe at the end of the lesson.

Wave Properties

Southern California

ENCOUNTER
THE PHENOMENON | Why can you feel thunder?

Sometimes thunder is loud and other times it is soft. What is the difference between loud and soft sounds? In the space below, write down observations on the different sounds in this activity.

Soft Sounds	Loud Sounds

Develop a list of questions that you would ask to find out more about soft and loud sounds. Write your questions in the space below.

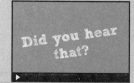

Did you hear that?

GO ONLINE
Watch the video *Did you hear that?* to see this phenomenon in action.

EXPLAIN
THE PHENOMENON

Rolling thunder. Time to seek shelter. The rain begins. Rumble. The thunder sounds louder this time. BOOM! The thunder rattles your home and you feel vibrations. You cannot see thunder. How is possible that thunder, a sound, can be felt? Use what you've observed to make a claim about why you can see or feel a wave.

CLAIM

A wave you see or feel is the result of...

COLLECT EVIDENCE as you work through the lesson. Then
return to these pages to record your evidence.

EVIDENCE

A. What evidence have you discovered to describe a wave?

B. What evidence have you discovered to explain how energy affects a wave?

MORE EVIDENCE

C. What evidence have you discovered to explain how the shape of a wave changes as the source of the wave changes?

When you are finished with the lesson, review your evidence. If necessary, based on the evidence, revise your claim.

REVISED CLAIM

A wave you see or feel is the result of...

Finally, explain your reasoning for how and why your evidence supports your claim.

REASONING

The evidence I collected supports my claim because...

What is a wave?

What do a clap of thunder and the ocean crashing on the shore have in common? They are both types of waves. You cannot make thunder or create an ocean wave, but you have created waves before. If you have ever clapped your hands or tossed a pebble into water, you have made a wave. Let's investigate to find out the characteristics of a wave.

Want more information?
Go online to read more about wave properties.

LAB Making Waves

Safety

Materials

coiled spring toy
tape
string
scissors
tape measure

Procedure

1. Read and complete a lab safety form.

2. Use tape to secure one end of a spring toy to your desk and the other end to the floor. Tie pieces of string to the spring 1/4, 1/2, and 3/4 of the way between the floor and the desk.

3. Pull a few of the lowest coils on the spring toy to the right. Release. Record your observations on the next page in the Data and Observations section.

4. Slowly tap the bottom of the spring toward the right. Repeat, this time doubling your rate of tapping. Record your observations.

5. Push down the bottom 5 cm of the spring toy. Release. Repeat, this time pushing down the bottom 10 cm. Record your observations.

6. Draw the waves on the next page under the data table.

7. Follow your teacher's instructions for proper cleanup.

Data and Observations

Displacement	Movement of Strings	Movement of Spring Toy
Pulled right and released		
Tapped slowly to the right		
Tapped quickly to the right		
Compressed bottom 5 cm		
Compressed bottom 10 cm		

Wave drawings

Analyze and Conclude

8. What patterns did you notice when you pulled the spring toy to the right? How was that similar to compressing the spring?

_____

_____

_____

_____

9. Compare the movement of the pieces of string in steps 4 and 5.

_____

_____

_____

_____

10. What conclusion can you draw between the amount of energy used to make a wave and its physical observations?

_____

_____

_____

_____

Waves A **wave** is a disturbance that transfers energy from one place to another without transferring matter. In the Lab *Making Waves,* the coil spring moved because your hand transferred energy to the spring.

All waves have an energy source. In the *Making Waves* lab, the source of energy came from your hand. In the photo on the right, the impact of the raindrops on the water is the source of energy for these water waves. Waves transfer energy away from the source of the energy. The source of energy is also known as a vibration. A vibration is a back-and-forth or an up-and-down movement of an object. Vibrating objects, such as a drum or a guitar string, are the sources of energy that produce sound waves.

Mechanical Waves The waves you just investigated transferred energy from one place to another without transferring any matter. Waves made with coiled spring toys, sound waves, and ocean waves are all mechanical waves. A **mechanical wave** is a wave that travels only through matter. Mechanical waves can travel through solids, liquids, and gases, but not through a vacuum. A material in which a wave travels is called a **medium.**

Monterey, CA

Transverse Waves Two types of mechanical waves are transverse waves and longitudinal waves. You created transverse waves in steps 3 and 4 of the Lab *Making Waves*. A **transverse wave** is a wave in which the disturbance is perpendicular to the direction the wave travels. Examples of transverse waves include a flag moving in the wind. Now, look at the figure below. Notice the repeating pattern of crests and troughs as the rope moves up and down away from its rest position. The wave travels from the hand to the doorknob as the rope moves up and down.

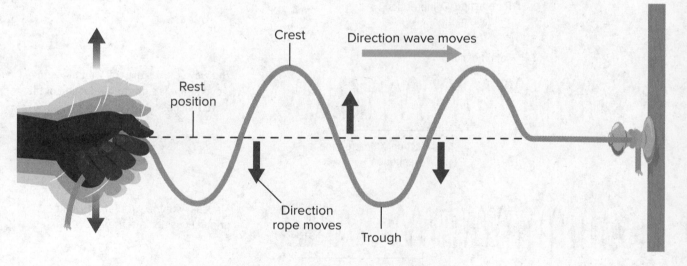

Crest

Direction wave moves

Rest position

Direction rope moves

Trough

Suppose you moved the end of a coil spring down, up, and back down to its original position. The up-and-down movement of your hand is one vibration. One vibration of your hand produces a transverse wave with one crest and one trough.

Now imagine that you move the end of the coil spring up and down several times. The motion of your hand transfers energy to the coil spring and produces several crests and troughs. As long as your hand keeps moving up and down, energy transfers to the coil spring and produces waves. When your hand stops, waves no longer are produced. However, the waves produced by the earlier movements of your hand continue to travel along the spring. This is true for any vibrating object. Waves can keep moving even after the object stops vibrating.

Longitudinal Waves You created longitudinal waves in step 5 of the Lab *Making Waves*. A **longitudinal wave** causes the particles in a medium to move parallel to the direction that the wave travels. Look at the figures below. Notice the wave produces regions in the spring where the coils are closer together than they are in the rest position and regions where they are farther apart. The sections of a longitudinal wave where the particles in the medium are closest together are compressions. The regions of a longitudinal wave where the particles are farthest apart are rarefactions.

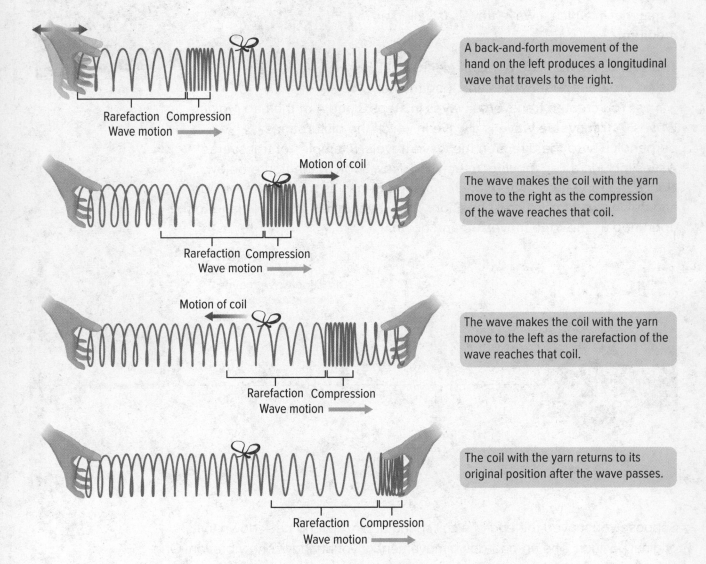

Rarefaction Compression
Wave motion →

A back-and-forth movement of the hand on the left produces a longitudinal wave that travels to the right.

Motion of coil →

Rarefaction Compression
Wave motion →

The wave makes the coil with the yarn move to the right as the compression of the wave reaches that coil.

← Motion of coil

Rarefaction Compression
Wave motion →

The wave makes the coil with the yarn move to the left as the rarefaction of the wave reaches that coil.

Rarefaction Compression
Wave motion →

The coil with the yarn returns to its original position after the wave passes.

Sound Waves One type of longitudinal wave is a sound wave. A **sound wave** is a longitudinal wave that can travel only through matter. The sounds you might hear now are traveling through air—a mixture of solids and gases. When swimming, you may have dove underwater and heard someone call to you. Then the sound waves traveled through a liquid. Sound waves travel through a solid when you knock on a door. Sound is produced by a vibration. As the vibration of the door occurs, the door collides with nearby air particles. The door transfers energy to those particles. The air particles collide with other air particles carrying energy outward from the source.

Sound Wave Models A coiled spring toy shows the properties of a longitudinal wave. Sound wave models show how the air particles move as the energy from the sound wave travels through the air. Look at the figure below. Each time the speaker cone moves forward, it pushes air particles ahead of it in the room.

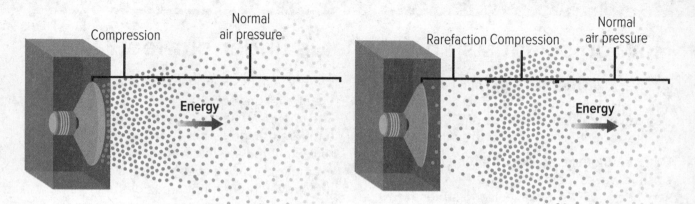

When the speaker cone moves out, it forces particles in the air closer together. This produces a high-pressure area, or compression.

When the speaker cone moves back, it leaves behind an area with fewer particles. This is a low-pressure area called a rarefaction.

Water Waves Friction between the wind at sea and the water forms water waves. Energy from the wind transfers to the water as the water moves toward land. Like all waves, water waves only transport energy. Because the waves move only through matter, water waves are mechanical waves.

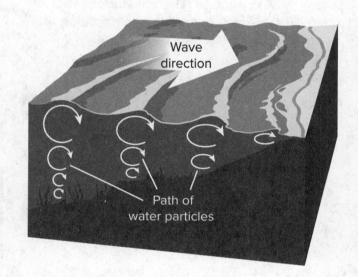

Although water waves look like transverse waves, water particles move in circles. Water waves are a combination of transverse and longitudinal waves. Water particles move forward and backward. They also move up and down. The result is a circular path that gets smaller as the wave approaches land.

EARTH SCIENCE Connection When layers of rock of Earth's crust suddenly shift, an earthquake occurs. The movement of rock rapidly releases energy along the fault. This sends out waves that travel to Earth's surface. An earthquake wave is called a seismic wave. There are different types of seismic waves. Seismic waves are mechanical waves because they move through matter.

COLLECT EVIDENCE

How can you describe a wave produced by thunder? Record your evidence (A) in the chart at the beginning of the lesson.

At the CORE of It

How do scientists know what is under our feet?

Did you know that the seismic waves that shake the ground during an earthquake also travel through the layers of Earth? This enables scientists to map Earth's interior.

Every earthquake produces three types of seismic waves: primary waves (P-waves), secondary waves (S-waves), and surface waves. Surface waves only travel along Earth's surface. P-waves and S-waves pass through Earth's interior. For this reason, they are also called body waves. By examining the behavior of body waves moving through different kinds of rock, scientists have determined the composition of layers all the way to Earth's inner core.

Seismic waves change speed and direction as they travel through the different layers of Earth. The speeds of seismic waves depend on the temperature, pressure, and chemistry of the rocks that the seismic waves travel through. For example, seismic waves tend to slow down as they travel through hot areas of the mantle beneath mid-ocean ridges or near hotspots. Seismic waves are faster in cool areas of the mantle near subduction zones.

What happens when they reach the core? When P-waves strike the core, they bend. S-waves—which cannot move through liquid—do not travel through Earth's center. This observation provided evidence that Earth's core must be at least partially liquid. The data collected for the paths and travel times of the waves inside Earth led to the current understanding that Earth's core has an outer region that is liquid and an inner region that is solid.

P-waves are longitudinal waves. They squeeze and push rocks in the direction along which the waves are traveling.

Wave direction

Particle movement

S-waves are transverse waves. They have a motion that causes rocks to move perpendicular to the direction of the waves.

Wave direction

Wave direction

Surface waves are a combination of longitudinal and transverse waves. They have back-and-forth motion as well as up-and-down or side-to-side motion.

Particle movement

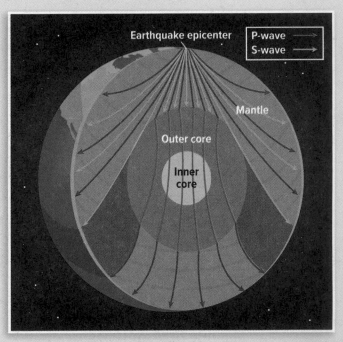

Earthquake epicenter

P-wave →
S-wave →

Mantle

Outer core

Inner core

Copyright © McGraw-Hill Education

It's Your Turn

EARTH SCIENCE ⟩ Connection Suppose you were on the team of scientists that first recognized that S-waves did not travel through Earth's outer core. Write an article for a science journal about your discovery.

How does energy affect a wave?

When you hear thunder, sometimes it is a low, soft rumble. Other times it is a strong, loud boom that rattles the windows. What causes the thunder to be different? Let's investigate!

FOLDABLES

Go to the Foldables® library to make a Foldable® that will help you take notes while reading this lesson.

 **LAB** Strike That

Safety

Materials

waxed paper

beaker

grains of rice

pencil

rubber band

Procedure

1. Read and complete a lab safety form.

2. Stretch waxed paper over the top of a beaker. Wrap a rubber band around the top to hold it tight.

3. Strike the center of the waxed paper gently with the eraser end of a pencil. Then strike it harder. How did the sound change? Write your observations in the Data and Observations section below.

4. Sprinkle a few grains of rice onto the waxed paper. Strike the paper gently and then harder. Observe how the rice moves each time. Record your observations.

5. Follow your teacher's instructions for proper cleanup.

Data and Observations

Analyze and Conclude

6. Contrast the waves made by tapping the pencil gently and then harder.

7. When did the pencil transfer more energy to the waxed paper? Explain your answer.

_____

_____

_____

_____

8. How are the loudness of the sounds and the energy of the strikes related?

_____

_____

_____

Amplitude and Energy Think back to when you struck the tuning fork sharply in the activity at the beginning of the lesson. A loud sound was produced. Placing the loud, vibrating tuning fork into the bowl of water produced waves with higher crests and deeper troughs than the softly vibrating tuning fork. This means the loud tuning fork caused water to move a greater distance from its rest position, producing a wave with a greater amplitude. The **amplitude** of a wave is the maximum distance that the wave moves from its rest position.

Proportional Relationships Examine the figure below. The transverse wave produced on the top has a smaller amplitude and carries less energy than the wave on the bottom. This models what you observed with the water in the activity at the beginning of the lesson. The square of the amplitude of a wave is proportional to the energy that produces the wave. Notice that each wave below has a repeating pattern with a specific amplitude.

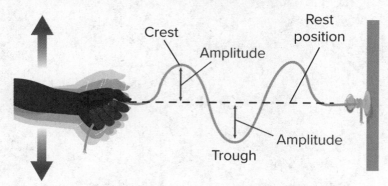

This wave has a smaller amplitude and carries less energy.

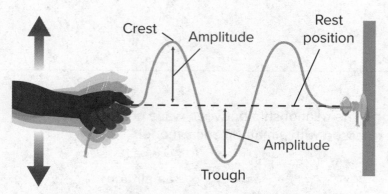

This wave has a greater amplitude and carries more energy.

Recall that a sound wave is longitudinal. Now, examine the figure below. This figure models how the sound waves behaved in the Lab *Strike That*. Just as for transverse waves, the energy carried by a longitudinal wave increases as its amplitude increases. The amplitude and energy are proportional. The low rumble of thunder has less energy and therefore, a smaller amplitude, than the loud boom of thunder.

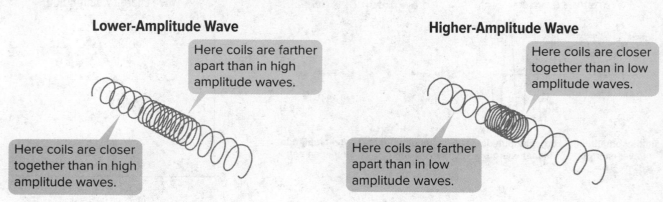

Lower-Amplitude Wave

Here coils are farther apart than in high amplitude waves.

Here coils are closer together than in high amplitude waves.

Higher-Amplitude Wave

Here coils are closer together than in low amplitude waves.

Here coils are farther apart than in low amplitude waves.

THREE-DIMENSIONAL THINKING

During a large thunderstorm, you hear and feel the thunder. Draw a representation of the sound wave produced. Your **model** should account for the energy and patterns of the wave.

MATH Connection The relationship between wave energy and amplitude can be expressed with a mathematical model.

$$\text{energy} \propto \text{amplitude}^2$$
$$E \propto A^2$$

This means that the energy of the wave is nonlinear. The energy of the wave is the square of the amplitude. For example, if the height is doubled, each wave will have four times the energy. If the height is halved, each wave will have a quarter of the energy. The figures below show the graphical and particle representations of this relationship.

Transverse wave

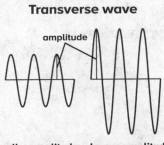

Smaller amplitude, lower energy   Larger amplitude, higher energy

Longitudinal wave

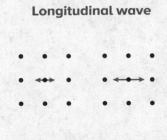

Smaller amplitude, lower energy   Larger amplitude, higher energy

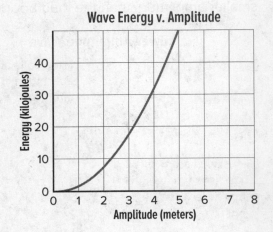

Wave Energy v. Amplitude

Copyright © McGraw-Hill Education

Read a Scientific Text

EARTH SCIENCE ▶ **Connection** A tsunami is a wave that forms when an ocean disturbance suddenly moves a large volume of water. The tsunami waves travel in all directions like waves that form when you drop a pebble into a pond. Most tsunamis are not a larger version of ocean waves on a normal day. A tsunami is generally very fast moving and reaches the shore much like the tide coming in. A powerful tsunami can travel inland up to 300 m.

CLOSE READING

Inspect

Read the passage from *Life of a Tsunami.*

Find Evidence

Reread the passage. Underline how the wave properties of the tsunami change as it approaches the shore.

Make Connections

Communicate With your partner, discuss how the energy of the tsunami changes as the tsunami reaches land. Use the changes of the wave properties to assist your conclusions.

PRIMARY SOURCE

Life of a Tsunami

Initiation: [...][N]ear the source of submarine earthquakes, the seafloor is "permanently" uplifted and down-dropped, pushing the entire water column up and down. The potential energy that results from pushing water above mean sea level is then transferred to horizontal propagation of the tsunami wave (kinetic energy). [...]

Split: Within several minutes of the earthquake, the initial tsunami [...] is split into a tsunami that travels out to the deep ocean (distant tsunami) and another tsunami that travels towards the nearby coast (local tsunami). [...] The height above mean sea level of the two oppositely traveling tsunamis is approximately half that of the original tsunami. [...] The speed at which both tsunamis travel varies as the square root of the water depth. Therefore, the deep-ocean tsunami travels faster than the local tsunami near shore.

Amplification: Several things happen as the local tsunami travels over the continental slope. Most obvious is that the amplitude increases. In addition, the wavelength decreases. This results in steepening of the leading wave. [...] Note that the first part of the wave reaching the local shore is a trough, which will appear as the sea receding far from shore. This is a common natural warning sign for tsunamis.

Runup: Tsunami runup occurs when a peak in the tsunami wave travels from the near-shore region onto shore. Runup is a measurement of the height of the water onshore observed above a reference sea level. Except for the largest tsunamis, [...] most tsunamis do not result in giant breaking waves (like normal surf waves at the beach that curl over as they approach shore). Rather, they come in much like very strong and fast-moving tides (i.e., strong surges and rapid changes in sea level). Much of the damage inflicted by tsunamis is caused by strong currents and floating debris. [...] Tsunamis will often travel much farther inland than normal waves. Do tsunamis stop once on land? No! After runup, part of the tsunami energy is reflected back to the open ocean and scattered by sharp variations in the coastline.

Source: U.S. Geological Survey

Amplitude and Loudness The more energy a thunder clap has, the larger the amplitude, and the louder the sound will seem. **Loudness** is how you perceive the energy of a sound wave. Does thunder sound the same to you as it does to your friend who lives three miles away? Let's explore.

LAB Don't Be Alarmed

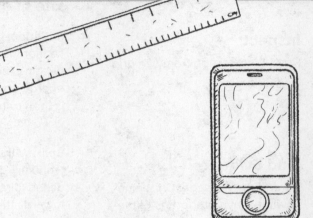

Safety

Materials

smartphone
sound-level meter
metric ruler

Procedure

1. Read and complete a lab safety form.

2. Increase the ring volume to maximum on a smartphone.

3. Place the smartphone 10 cm from the sound-level meter.

4. Ring the smartphone by using the alarm function and observe the reading on the sound-level meter. Record the reading in the Data and Observations section.

5. Repeat step 4 with the smartphone at a distance of 30 cm.

6. Repeat step 4 with the smartphone at a distance of 50 cm.

7. Follow your teacher's instructions for proper cleanup.

Data and Observations

Analyze and Conclude

8. Use your evidence to compare the loudness at the three positions.

_____

_____

_____

_____

9. Determine the relationship between the amount of energy of a sound wave and the distance.

_____

_____

_____

Amplitude, Intensity, and Loudness The smartphone alarm got quieter as it was moved farther away from the sound-level meter. As the particles of air in front of the phone vibrated back and forth, they collided with, and transferred energy to, surrounding particles of air. As the energy spread out among more and more air particles, the intensity of the wave decreased. **Intensity** is the amount of sound energy that passes through a square meter of space in one second.

As a sound wave travels farther from the phone, there is a larger area of air particles sharing the same amount of energy that left the phone. Therefore, the farther the smartphone was from the sound-level meter, the less energy passed through one square meter. This resulted in less intensity of the wave. As intensity decreased, amplitude decreased. Therefore, loudness decreased.

The unit decibel (dB) describes the intensity and, in turn, the loudness of sound. Decibel levels of common sounds are shown to the right. Each increase of 10 dB causes a sound about twice as loud. As the decibel level goes up, the amount of time you can listen to the sound without risking hearing loss gets shorter.

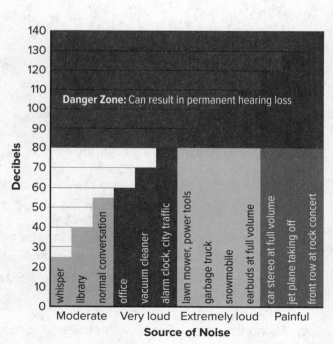

EXPLORE/EXPLAIN Lesson 1 Wave Properties   **23**

COLLECT EVIDENCE

In what ways does energy affect a wave? Record your evidence (B) in the chart at the beginning of the lesson.

How does the shape of a wave change as the source of the wave changes?

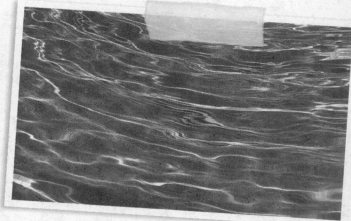

You have modeled soft sounds and loud sounds now in two activities. You understand that the more energy a wave has, the larger its amplitude. You also understand that as amplitude increases, the loudness, and therefore the intensity increases. What does that wave model look like? Let's investigate!

LAB Ride the Wave

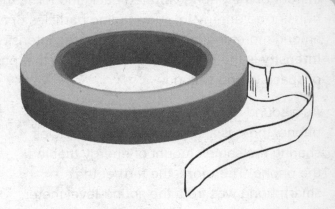

Safety

Materials

measuring tapes (2)

masking tape

coiled spring toy

stopwatch

Procedure

1. Read and complete a lab safety form.

2. With a partner, use masking tape to secure the measuring tapes to the floor, creating x- and y-axes in the shape of a T.

3. With your partner, stretch the spring toy across the measuring tape representing the x-axis. Generate a transverse wave by moving the toy back and forth on the floor. Try to be as steady and even as possible to generate consistent waves.

4. Using the measuring tape on the y-axis, measure and record the amplitude of the wave in the Data and Observations section on the next page.

5. Using the measuring tape representing the *x*-axis, measure from one crest to the next crest. Then measure from one trough to the next trough. Record your measurements.

6. Using a stopwatch, count and record the number of crests or troughs that cross the *y*-axis in 10 seconds.

7. Repeat steps 3–6 for waves with different properties by moving the toy faster and slower.

8. Follow your teacher's instructions for proper cleanup.

Data and Observations

Trial	Amplitude (cm)	Distance Between Crest and Next Crest	Distance Between Trough and Next Trough	Number of Vibrations in 10 Seconds
1				
2				
3				
4				

Analyze and Conclude

9. What pattern did you notice between the measurements from crest-to-crest and the measurements from trough-to-trough of the same trial?

_____

_____

_____

_____

10. Describe the relationship between the number of times the wave crossed the *y*-axis and the distance between two crests or two troughs.

_____

_____

_____

_____

Analyze and Conclude, continued

11. Explain how the energy was or was not proportional to the amplitude of the wave.

_____

_____

_____

_____

Wavelength You measured transverse waves from one crest to the next and from one trough to the next in the Lab *Ride the Wave*. The distance between one point on a wave to the same point on the next wave is the **wavelength.** Longitudinal waves are measured from one compression to the next compression or from one rarefaction to the next rarefaction. View the figure below to see the differences between the two wavelengths. For either wave type, the wavelength repeats as long as the energy remains constant. Wavelength is measured in units of distance, such as meters.

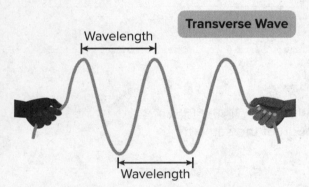

Wavelength is the distance from one crest to the next crest or from one trough to the next trough.

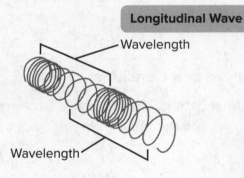

Wavelength is the distance from one compression to the next compression or from one rarefaction to the next rarefaction.

Frequency Waves have another property called frequency. The **frequency** of a wave is the number of times the pattern repeats in a given time. Frequency is related to how rapidly the object or material producing the wave vibrates. Each vibration of the object produces one wavelength. The frequency of a wave is the same as the number of vibrations the vibrating object makes each second. The SI unit for frequency is hertz (Hz). A wave with a frequency of 2 Hz means that two wavelengths pass a point each second. The unit Hz is the same unit as 1/s.

The amount of energy transferred by waves in a given time is proportional to the wave's frequency. If the frequency of the waves doubles, the energy of the wave also doubles. Similarly, if the frequency decreases by half, the energy will also decrease by half.

Wavelength and Frequency The properties of waves are not independent of each other. Look back at the table you completed in the Lab *Ride the Wave*. Your data should have indicated a strong relationship between wavelength and frequency. The figure below shows how frequency and wavelength are related. The wavelength of the wave in the left column is longer than that of the wave in the right column.

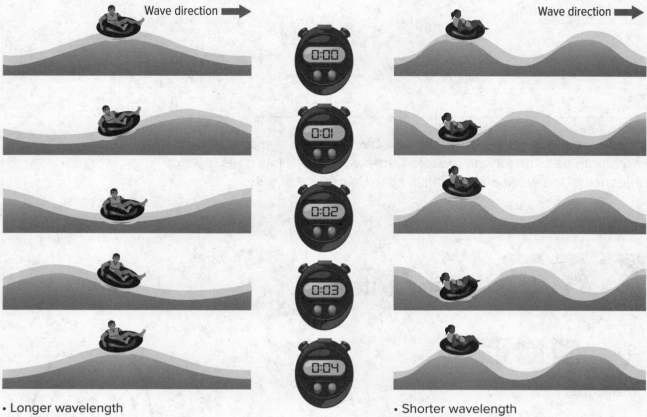

- Longer wavelength
- Lower frequency
- One complete wave passes in four seconds.

- Shorter wavelength
- Higher frequency
- Two complete waves pass in four seconds.

To calculate the frequency of waves, divide the number of wavelengths by the time. For the wave on the left, the frequency is 1 wavelength divided by 4 s, which is 0.25 Hz. The wave on the right has a frequency of 0.5 Hz. The wave on the right has a shorter wavelength and a higher frequency. As the frequency of a wave increases, the wavelength decreases.

MATH Connection You can express the relationship of wavelength and frequency with ratios. The wave on the left has a ratio of 1:4 wavelength to frequency. For every one wavelength, four seconds passed. What would the ratio be for two waves that traveled a total of 12 seconds?

THREE-DIMENSIONAL THINKING

What effect does increasing the number of vibrations have on the frequency and wavelength of a wave? What effect does decreasing the vibrations have on frequency and wavelength? Which change has more energy? Explain.

_____

_____

_____

_____

Sound Frequency In the Lab *Ride the Wave*, you saw that as the wavelength became longer, the frequency was lower. How does the frequency of the wave affect what is heard? Let's investigate!

 **LAB** Fever Pitch

Safety

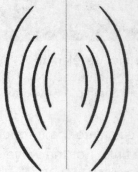

Materials

measuring tape   string
scissors

Procedure

1. Read and complete a lab safety form.

2. Use scissors to cut a piece of string 1 m long. Attach one end securely to the leg of a desk.

3. Hold the other end of the string and stretch it horizontally. Pluck the string several times. What do you notice?

_____

4. Hold the string at various lengths and pluck it. Notice how the sounds differ.

5. Next, hold the string at the lengths listed in the data table on the next page. Observe how the sound changes as you pull the string with a weaker force and then with a stronger force. Record your observations.

6. Follow your teacher's instructions for proper cleanup.

Data and Observations

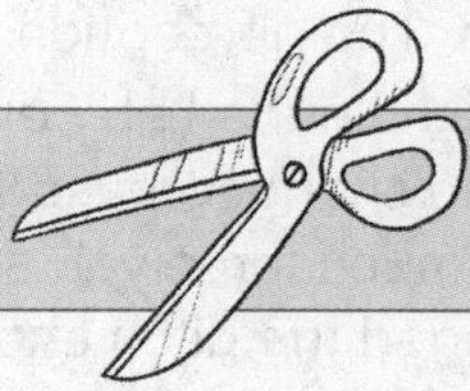

Length of string plucked	Force	Observations
90 cm	weak	
45 cm	weak	
22.5 cm	weak	
90 cm	strong	
45 cm	strong	
22.5 cm	strong	

Analyze and Conclude

7. Describe the patterns you observed.

_____

_____

_____

8. Using your evidence, explain how the frequency, wavelength, amplitude, and energy changed as the sound changed.

_____

_____

_____

_____

_____

_____

_____

Pitch The perception of how high or low a sound seems is **pitch.** In the Lab *Fever Pitch* you determined that the sound changed based on how long the string was and by how much force you applied. The length of the string changed the pitch and the frequency. Recall that frequency is the number of times the pattern repeats in a given amount of time. When talking about sound waves, frequency is often referred to as beats per second.

A higher frequency produces a higher pitch. For example, an adult male voice might range from 85 Hz to 155 Hz. An adult female voice might range from about 165 Hz to 255 Hz. Humans can hear thunder frequencies between 20 Hz and 120 Hz.

The human ear can detect sounds with frequencies between about 20 Hz and 20,000 Hz. Frequencies above this range are called ultrasound. The range of sounds heard by various animals is shown in figure to the right.

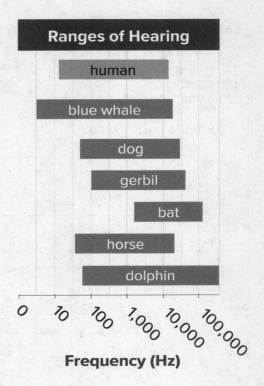

Ranges of Hearing

human · blue whale · dog · gerbil · bat · horse · dolphin

Frequency (Hz)
0 · 10 · 100 · 1,000 · 10,000 · 100,000

THREE-DIMENSIONAL THINKING

Create wave **models** to represent physical observations of patterns of sound. Draw three illustrations 1) tires squealing—a loud and high-pitched sound, 2) thunder—a loud and low-pitched sound, and 3) mosquito buzz—a quiet but high-pitched sound.

COLLECT EVIDENCE

How does the source of a wave change the shape? Record your evidence (C) in the chart at the beginning of the lesson.

Cochlear Implants

Helping Damaged Ears Hear Again

Is there any way to hear again after hair cells in your cochlea are destroyed? Not long ago, the answer was no. But over the last 20 to 30 years, scientists developed a way to bypass the damaged cells. It is called a cochlear implant—a device that uses electrical signals to stimulate the nerves that go from the ear to the brain. How does it work? First a surgeon implants the interior part of the device under the scalp and into the inner ear. Then the exterior part of the device is put to work. With hearing restored, you are once again connected to the sounds in the world around you!

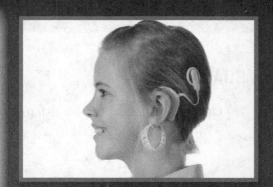

1. **A microphone receives sound waves from the environment. A speech processor changes sounds into electrical signals.**

2. **The electrical signals are then sent across the scalp from the transmitter to a receiver.**

3. **The receiver sends the signals through a wire to electrodes implanted in the cochlea.**

4. **Nerves in the inner ear pick up the signals and send them to the brain. The brain interprets the signals as sound.**

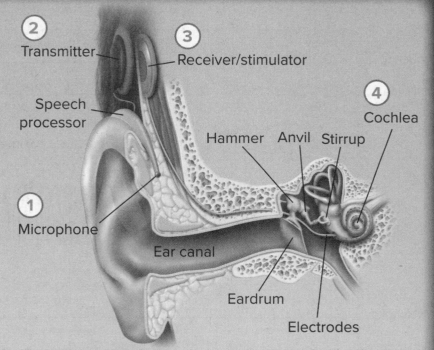

(2) Transmitter
(3) Receiver/stimulator
Speech processor
(4) Cochlea
Hammer   Anvil   Stirrup
(1) Microphone
Ear canal
Eardrum
Electrodes

It's Your Turn

READING Connection How is a hearing aid similar and how is it different from a cochlear implant? Research both devices. Compare how sound travels in these devices to what you learned about how sound travels in the lesson. Create a slideshow presentation to share what you've discovered.

Review

Summarize It!

1. **Determine** the wavelength, frequency, and amplitude for each wave.

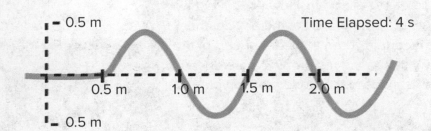

Wavelength: _____

Frequency: _____

Amplitude: _____

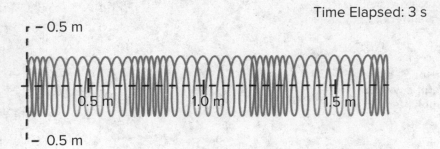

Wavelength: _____

Frequency: _____

Amplitude: _____

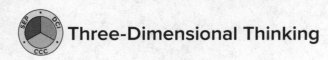
Three-Dimensional Thinking

2. Joni plays a scale on her clarinet. As she plays from low notes to high notes, what happens to the sound waves that the clarinet creates?

    A   The amplitude of the sound waves decreases.

    B   The frequency of the sound waves increases.

    C   The intensity of the sound waves increases.

    D   The wavelengths of the sound waves increase.

Sound	Decibel Level
Tornado siren	140 dB
Jackhammer	130 dB
Chain saw	100 dB
Lawn mower	90 dB
Vacuum cleaner	75 dB
Dishwasher	60 dB

3. The table above shows the decibels produced by a number of objects. According to the table, which sound has 1,000 times more energy than the sound of a dishwasher?

    A   chain saw

    B   jackhammer

    C   lawn mower

    D   tornado siren

Real-World Connection

4. Analyze You are with a friend in the schoolyard. You rest your ear against a metal leg of the swings while your friend gently taps on the leg. You hear the tapping. Describe the wave produced by tapping. Is it a longitudinal wave or a transverse wave? Draw a model of the wave.

5. Evaluate Surfers often enjoy riding big waves. Using what you have learned about waves and energy, explain why it is harder to ride big waves than to ride small waves. Cite evidence to support your reasoning.

 Still have questions?
Go online to check your understanding about wave properties.

REVISIT  **PAGE KEELEY SCIENCE PROBES**

Do you still agree with the person you chose at the beginning of the lesson? Return to the Science Probe at the beginning of the lesson. Explain why you agree or disagree with that person now.

EXPLAIN THE PHENOMENON

Revisit your claim about what waves you can see or hear result from. Review the evidence you collected. Explain how your evidence supports your claim.

START PLANNING

STEM Module Project Engineering Challenge

Now that you understand how the properties of waves relate to physical observations, go to your Module Project to research how the properties of water waves can cause damage to beaches. Keep in mind what happens when you are hit by a wave.

PERFORMANCE EXPECTATION

Tin Can Phone

Addison showed Rachel a phone that her grandmother helped her make. It was two cans connected with a string. Addison kept one can and gave the other can to Rachel. Next, the two friends walked away from each other until the string was tight. Then Addison spoke into her can, while Rachel held her can to her ear. Rachel could hear Addison. Why did this work?

A.   The energy of the sound wave is absorbed by the string.

B.   The energy of the sound wave is reflected by the string.

C.   The energy of the sound wave is transmitted by the string.

D.   The energy is not related to sound waves.

Circle the statement you most agree with. Explain why you agree with that statement.

_____

_____

_____

You will revisit your response to the Science Probe at the end of the lesson.

Mechanical Wave Interactions

ENCOUNTER
THE PHENOMENON

Why are the walls of a recording studio covered in foam?

Listen to the sounds being played in your classroom. Draw a model of the sound waves coming from the device.

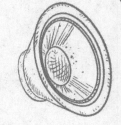

Listen to the sounds coming from the device when it is placed inside a right-side up glass. Draw a model of the sound waves coming from the device.

Listen to the sounds coming from the device when it is placed inside an upside down glass. Draw a model of the sound waves coming from the device.

Right Back at You

▶

GO ONLINE

Watch the video *Right Back at You* to see this phenomenon in action.

EXPLAIN
THE PHENOMENON

Look around your classroom. Most likely the walls are flat. In fact, almost all walls are flat. Recording studios are different. They can have a variety of shapes and materials on the walls. Use what you've observed to make a claim about why recording studios have foam on the walls.

CLAIM

Recording studios have foam on the walls because...

 COLLECT EVIDENCE as you work through the lesson. Then return to these pages to record your evidence.

EVIDENCE

A. What evidence have you discovered to explain how a wave travels through matter?

MORE EVIDENCE

B. What evidence have you discovered to explain how a wave interacts with matter?

When you are finished with the lesson, review your evidence. If necessary, based on the evidence, revise your claim.

REVISED CLAIM

Recording studios have foam on the walls because...

Finally, explain your reasoning for how and why your evidence supports your claim.

REASONING

The evidence I collected supports my claim because...

How do waves interact with matter?

In the activity, did you notice a difference in how the sound wave sounded as the conditions it was played under changed? How did the sound waves interact with the glass? Think about a time you created a water wave. What happened when the wave hit the sides of the container? Did the way the wave interacted with the surrounding matter change the wave's properties? Let's investigate!

 Want more information?
Go online to read more about mechanical wave interactions.

FOLDABLES

Go to the Foldables® library to make a Foldable® that will help you take notes while reading this lesson.

LAB Crashing Waves

Safety 🥽 🧤 🧼

Materials

clear, rectangular pan
sponges cut into thin strips
interlocking plastic blocks
adhesive putty
2-cm wooden dowel
books (2)
white paper
water

Procedure

1. Read and complete a lab safety form.

2. Make a ripple tank by placing two equal-height books under the short edges of the pan. Secure the edges with putty. Slide a sheet of white paper under the pan. Lay strips of sponge inside the short ends of the pan to absorb wave energy. Lay the dowel in one of the short ends of the pan. Pour water into the pan until it is about 1 cm deep.

3. Tap the dowel with your finger to make a series of waves. Observe properties of the waves. Increase and decrease the wavelength of your waves. Explain in the Data and Observations section how you changed the wavelength.

4. Make a barrier from interlocking blocks. The barrier should be approximately 15 cm long. Lay the barrier in your ripple tank at approximately a 45° angle to the dowel. What will happen to waves that hit against the barrier? Try it, and then change the angle of the barrier and repeat. Record your observations with words and images.

5. Follow your teacher's instructions for proper cleanup.

Data and Observations

Analyze and Conclude

6. When the waves left the dowel and came in contact with the sponge at the opposite end, how did the amplitude change?

_____

_____

_____

_____

Analyze and Conclude, continued

7. How did changing the barriers' angle change the waves?

_____

_____

_____

_____

⟩ GO ONLINE for additional opportunities to explore!

Investigate wave interactions by performing one of the following activities.

☐ **Model** additional ripple tank setups in the **PhET Interactive Simulation** *Wave Interference*.

OR

☐ **Model** sound wave interactions with a barrier in the **PhET Interactive Simulation** *Sound*.

Interaction of Waves with Matter Did you notice in the Lab *Crashing Waves* that when the wave hit the barrier it bounced back? As the wave moved it carried energy. When it hit the barrier, the energy reflected, or bounced back. **Reflection** is the bouncing of a wave off a surface. All waves reflect. An echo is an example of a sound wave reflecting. Ocean waves reflect off boats, islands, and piers.

When a wave reflects, it changes direction. You saw this in the Lab *Crashing Waves*. When the wave you created with the dowel came in contact with the barrier, the wave changed direction. As you changed the angle of the barrier, the wave reflected back at an angle different from the previous time. The direction the wave hits the barrier and the direction of the reflected wave are related. When a wave is reflected from a surface, the angle of the reflection is equal to the angle the wave strikes the barrier.

Absorption Did you notice that the wave that reflected off the barrier in the Lab *Crashing Waves* was not as big as the first wave you made? After a while the wave would stop bouncing off of surfaces and it would disappear. What happened to the energy the wave was carrying? Sometimes when a wave hits a barrier, some of its energy is absorbed by the barrier. **Absorption** is the transfer of energy by a wave to the medium through which it travels. The amount of energy absorbed depends on the type of wave and the material in which it moves. In the figure on the right the sound from the cell phone is absorbed by the insulation in the wall.

Transmission You also might have noticed a small wave appear on the other side of the barrier in the Lab *Crashing Waves.* Sometimes when a wave interacts with matter, the matter does not absorb all of the energy. The matter can transmit some of the energy to the other side of the barrier and it will continue as a wave. **Transmission** is the passage of a wave through a medium. The sound from a cell phone in the figure on the right transmits easily through an uninsulated wall. Mechanical waves can also travel through liquids and gases. Without transmission we would not hear sound waves on the other side of doors.

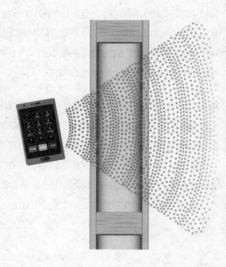

INVESTIGATION

It's All Material

Have you ever been in class when a large, noisy group goes down the hall? At first your teacher's voice probably rose. As the volume got louder, he likely closed the door. How do different materials affect the interactions of sound waves?

GO ONLINE Watch the animation *It's All Material.* Record your observations below.

_____

_____

_____

_____

1. How does the type of material affect how it will be used?

_____

_____

_____

MUSIC › Connection | Acoustical engineers must take into account the type of materials they are working with. If they are designing a concert hall, these engineers carefully choose the shapes and materials to control sound waves. The stage has a wooden floor to improve vibrations. The curved panels on the ceiling reflect sound waves in different directions to fill the space.

Highway sound barriers are another example of controlling sound waves. The barriers are often made from wood, concrete, or metal, like the one shown on the right. The barriers' purpose is to keep the highway noise away from residential areas. The higher the wall, the more sound will be reflected from the hard surface.

THREE-DIMENSIONAL THINKING

When a wave interacts with matter it can reflect the energy, absorb the energy, transmit the energy, or do all three. **Develop a model** using the figure below to describe the sound wave interactions with the materials in the room. Then, **construct an explanation** of how you would use structures to increase the absorption. Write your response in your Science Notebook.

LIFE SCIENCE › Connection Our sense of hearing is an interaction of waves with matter. Sound waves enter the ears with information about the environment. The sound waves interact with different mediums and structures within the ear as the waves move. The human ear has three main parts, as shown in the figure below.

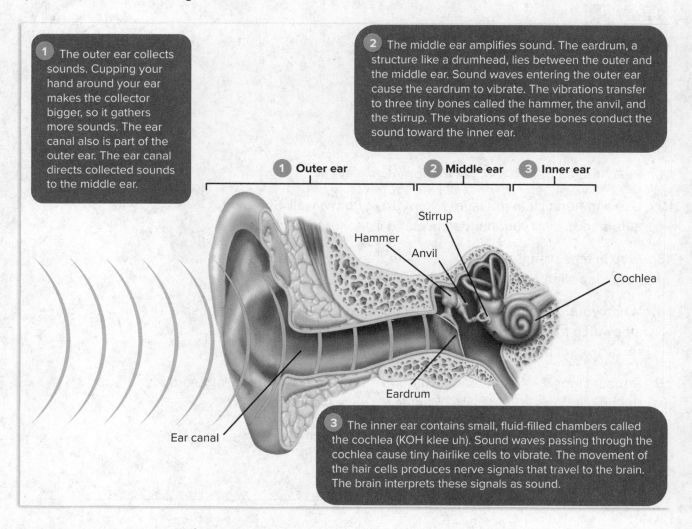

1 The outer ear collects sounds. Cupping your hand around your ear makes the collector bigger, so it gathers more sounds. The ear canal also is part of the outer ear. The ear canal directs collected sounds to the middle ear.

2 The middle ear amplifies sound. The eardrum, a structure like a drumhead, lies between the outer and the middle ear. Sound waves entering the outer ear cause the eardrum to vibrate. The vibrations transfer to three tiny bones called the hammer, the anvil, and the stirrup. The vibrations of these bones conduct the sound toward the inner ear.

1 Outer ear   **2** Middle ear   **3** Inner ear

Stirrup

Hammer

Anvil

Cochlea

Eardrum

Ear canal

3 The inner ear contains small, fluid-filled chambers called the cochlea (KOH klee uh). Sound waves passing through the cochlea cause tiny hairlike cells to vibrate. The movement of the hair cells produces nerve signals that travel to the brain. The brain interprets these signals as sound.

COLLECT EVIDENCE

How do waves interact with matter? Record your evidence (A) in the chart at the beginning of the lesson.

What affects how a wave travels through matter?

You've just explored reflection, absorption, and transmission. Do all waves interact the same way? Consider how quickly a water wave at the beach comes to shore. Think about how a car horn can be heard almost immediately. What would happen if you placed something between you and a microphone in the recording studio?

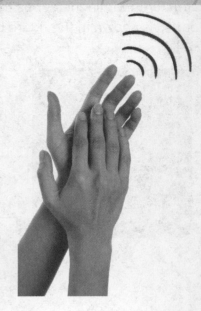

Safety

Materials

meterstick

stopwatch

Procedure

1. Read and complete a lab safety form.

2. Use a meterstick to measure a spot 30 m from a wall. Standing at this spot, clap your hands once and listen for the echo.

3. Clap in time with the echo. If you hear the echo after each clap, clap slightly faster.

4. When your clapping matches the echo speed, have your partner use a stopwatch to measure the time as you clap 25 times. Create a table and record your time in the Data and Observations section below.

5. Repeat steps 2–4 at distances of 40 m and 50 m from the wall. Record the time it takes you to clap 25 times for each distance.

6. Follow your teacher's instructions for proper cleanup.

Data and Observations

Copyright © McGraw-Hill Education   ersinkisacik/E+/Getty Images

Analyze and Conclude

7. The speed of sound can be calculated by dividing the distance by the time. Calculate the speed of sound for each distance.

8. If you performed this experiment on a cold day, the speed of the echo would be slower. Predict why the speed of the sound wave is less.

_____

_____

_____

_____

Speed of Sound In the Lab *Echo, echo!* you were able to calculate the speed of sound through air. Recall that for sound to be transmitted energy must pass from particle to particle. The material, or medium, that sound passes through affects how fast the sound moves. Two factors that influence the speed of sound waves are the density and the temperature of the medium.

Gas particles are far apart and collide less often than particles in a liquid or a solid. As shown in the table on the right, a gas takes longer to transfer sound energy between particles. In a solid where the particles are packed very close together, the particles collide and transfer energy very quickly. The more dense a medium, the faster sound will travel through it.

Particles move faster and collide more often as the temperature of a gas increases. This increase in the number of collisions transfers more energy in less time. Temperature has the opposite effect on liquids and sounds. As liquids and solids cool, the molecules move closer together. They collide more often and transfer energy faster.

The Speed of Sound	
Medium	**Speed (m/s)**
Air (0°C)	331
Air (20°C)	343
Water (20°C)	1,481
Water (0°C)	1,500
Seawater (25°C)	1,533
Ice (0°C)	3,500
Iron	5,130
Glass	5,640

LAB Breaking Waves

Materials

clear, rectangular pan
sponges cut into thin strips
interlocking plastic blocks
adhesive putty
2-cm wooden dowel
books (2)
white paper
water

Procedure

1. Read and complete a lab safety form.

2. Set up the ripple tank as in the Lab *Crashing Waves*.

3. Tap the dowel with your finger to make a series of waves. Observe how the waves are reflected, absorbed, or transmitted through the sponge at the opposite end. Record your observations in the Data and Observations section on the next page.

4. Increase the strength with which you tap the dowel. Record how the wave interactions changed.

5. Make two equal-length barriers from interlocking plastic blocks blocks. Place the barriers end-to-end in your ripple tank at approximately a 45° angle to the dowel. What will happen to waves that hit against the barrier? Try it, and then change the angle of the barrier and repeat. Record your observations with words and images.

6. Place the two barriers in the middle of the pan, parallel to the dowel, with a small space between the two parts. Make waves with different frequencies move through the space between the barriers. Observe how the waves change when they move through the space. Repeat, increasing the distance between the barriers. Record your observations with words and images.

7. Follow your teacher's instructions for proper cleanup.

Data and Observations

Analyze and Conclude

8. Place the barriers in a new formation in your tank. Predict the behavior of the waves. Draw a diagram of your setup and prediction. How well were you able to predict how the waves would behave?

Analyze and Conclude, continued

9. Contrast the wave behavior when the barriers were placed together and when the barriers had space between them.

_____

_____

_____

_____

Diffraction The waves in the Lab _Breaking Waves_ didn't break, but rather changed direction when they came to a barrier. The change in direction of a wave when it travels by the edge of an object or through an opening is called **diffraction.** Both water waves and sound waves diffract. You have experienced sound diffraction if you have ever been in a hallway and heard people talking in a room before you got to the open door of that room. Diffraction causes water waves to travel around the edges of the object and spread out after they travel through an opening—just like in the _Breaking Waves_ lab. More diffraction occurs as the size of the object or opening becomes similar in size to the wavelength of the wave.

THREE-DIMENSIONAL THINKING

Imagine you are conducting a new ripple tank experiment with two different barrier structures. The first time you make waves, the structure is a sponge. The second time it is a brick. Based on your previous observations, create an argument for which structure you think will have the most effect on frequency, amplitude, and wavelength.

_____

_____

_____

_____

_____

COLLECT EVIDENCE

What affects how a wave travels through matter? Record your evidence (B) in the chart at the beginning of the lesson.

A Day in the Life of a Surfboard Shaper

The earliest recorded history of surfing is from the late 1700s in Hawaii. Surf boards were made of wood and varied in length from 2.44 m to 7.32 m. The boards could weigh 45 kg! All the boards were made without power tools. Coral and stones were used to sand the wood. Various plant extracts and oils were used to treat and protect the boards.

Fast forward to today. Many surfboards are still made by hand. A surfboard shaper takes many factors into account when planning, including the surfer's height and weight, and the type of waves the surfer wants to ride. The shaper starts with a blank—an unrefined piece of foam. She uses a variety of planers and sanding machines to shape the board like in the photo above. When the shaper has finished shaping the blank, she applies fiberglass cloth to the board. The fiberglass gives the board strength. Once the fiberglass cloth is in place, resin is applied to bond the cloth to the foam. Multiple coats of resin are used. The resin makes the board waterproof.

It's Your Turn

WRITING Connection Surfboards have had many shapes and sizes since the late 1700s. Research two different boards. Draw evidence from your research to support analysis and reflection of why the board has its specific shape and size. Compare the materials they are made from as well their shapes. Write your results in the form of a blog. Use visuals to clarify your information and add interest. Include any questions you generated while researching.

Review

Summarize It!

1. **Describe** the ways waves interact. Create a model of each type of interaction.

Interaction	Description	Model
Reflection		
Absorption		
Transmission		
Diffraction		

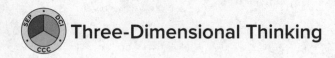 **Three-Dimensional Thinking**

Speed of Sound in Different Materials	
Material (at 20°C)	**Speed (m/s)**
Air	343
Glass	5,640
Iron	5,130
Water	1,481

2. A sound wave takes about 0.03 s to move through a material that is 10.3 m long. What is the material?

   A air

   B glass

   C iron

   D water

---

3. You are in a sound-proofed hallway. Someone standing around the corner from you speaks and you hear them. Which claim offers the best evidence and reasoning for this phenomenon?

   A Sound is not affected by types of materials, because sound can travel though solids, liquids, and gases.

   B Sound waves are absorbed by the sound-proofed walls and then transmitted through the wall to your ear.

   C Sound waves diffract so even though the walls do not reflect the sound wave, the sound wave can still travel to your ear.

   D Sound-proof walls allow sound waves to reflect all of the sound that is directed toward them. So the sound must bounce off them and go to your ear.

Real-World Connection

4. **Propose** An architect wants to design a conference room that reduces noise coming from outside the room. Suggest some design features, including their structure and function that should be considered in this project.

_____

_____

_____

_____

_____

_____

_____

_____

_____

_____

_____

 Still have questions?
Go online to check your understanding about mechanical wave interactions.

 **REVISIT SCIENCE PROBES**
Do you still agree with the statement you chose at the beginning of the lesson? Return to the Science Probe at the beginning of the lesson. Explain why you agree or disagree with that statement now.

EXPLAIN THE PHENOMENON

Revisit your claim about why recording studio walls are covered in foam. Review the evidence you collected. Explain how your evidence supports your claim.

PLAN AND PRESENT
STEM Module Project Engineering Challenge

Now that you understand how waves reflect, absorb, and transmit through materials, go to your Module Project and research technologies that are used to reduce wave damage on beaches. Keep in mind what happens when you are hit by a wave.

PERFORMANCE EXPECTATION

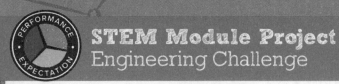
Don't Make Waves

Santa Barbara, CA

During the Atlantic hurricane season, videos of huge waves crashing against the shore are commonly seen on national weather reports. These waves are known to cause extensive beach damage to shorelines. Many coastal areas are known for their beaches, which are major tourism draws to their communities.

One coastal community is looking to install a preventive measure to reduce the damage to the beach caused by waves during storms. You have been selected to be a part of a committee that will evaluate different preventive designs. You will choose which design will be the most economical for your community, and build a model to demonstrate how the design will help protect the beach.

Planning After Lesson 1

Research how water waves can cause damage to beaches. Gather information from multiple print sources. Then, answer the questions using your knowledge from the lesson and your findings from your research.

Construct an explanation of how an increase in wave amplitude would affect beach damage. Use a model to support your explanation.

Planning After Lesson 1, continued

Construct an explanation of how an increase in wave frequency would affect beach damage. Use a model to support your explanation.

Planning After Lesson 2

Research technologies that are used to reduce the damage of waves hitting the shore. Record the questions and answers that drive your research in the space below. Include citations for your sources.

Organizing Data

Create a table that lists:
- each type of technology that was researched,
- how the technology reduces damage from waves, and
- the societal and environmental impacts of each technology.

Add columns to the table that identify each criteria and constraint. Use the table to evaluate the strengths and weaknesses of each technology.

Develop Another Model

Develop a physical model to illustrate how you would protect a shoreline from damage caused by waves. Be sure to identify the following components:

- type of waves (including wavelength and frequency),
- various materials through which the waves are reflected, absorbed, and transmitted,
- characteristics of the wave after it has interacted with a material, and
- position of the source of the wave.

In your model, identify and describe relationships between the components by highlighting the interactions of the waves with materials through reflection, absorption, and transmission.

Evaluate Your Design

As a group, develop a plan on how to investigate which technology best meets the criteria and constraints. In this plan include:

- What criteria and constraints will be used in the evaluation of the design solution?

- How will you use your knowledge of wave properties and interactions to determine how well the design solution meets the criteria and constraints?

Create tables to organize the data before testing the devices created by your class.

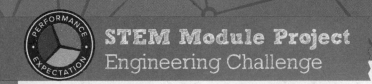

Create Your Presentation

Evaluate your model against the models of other groups. Make a claim about the relative effectiveness of the proposed solutions based on the strengths and weaknesses of each. Support your claim with evidence, and present your argument to the class.

Prepare a short presentation of your model for protecting a shoreline from waves. Use your model to make sense of the wave interactions of reflection, absorption, and transmission, and to describe how the properties of different components are well suited to certain functions associated with these interactions.

Congratulations! You've completed the Engineering Challenge requirements!

Module Wrap-Up

REVISIT
THE PHENOMENON

Using the concepts you learned throughout this module about wave properties and interactions, explain why a wave can knock you down.

INQUIRY

If you had to ask one question about what you studied, what would it be?

_____

_____

_____

_____

Plan and conduct an investigation to answer this question.

Light

ENCOUNTER
THE PHENOMENON

▌How do rainbows form?

Chasing Rainbows

▶ GO ONLINE
Watch the video *Chasing Rainbows* to see this phenomenon in action.

Collaborate With a partner, develop a list of questions that you could investigate to find out more about how rainbows form. Record your questions below.

Optical Illusions

A famous illusionist has hired you to design a new type of optical illusion for a show. How will you do it? To make an optical illusion, you have to use light to make people see an image that is not really there. Here is your challenge:

- You may use only common materials and devices approved by your teacher.

- You must use at least two different interactions of light.

- The image you create must be different from the object(s) in at least two ways (for example, size, orientation, color, or position).

You will then need to develop and use a model to describe how the illusion works as a result of light wave interactions with various materials.

Start Thinking About It

In the photo above there are two frogs. One is real and one is an illusion. Which frog is the real frog? How do you think the illusion frog is made? Discuss your thoughts with your group.

STEM Module Project

Planning and Completing the Engineering Challenge How will you meet this goal? The concepts you will learn throughout this module will help you plan and complete the Engineering Challenge. Just follow the prompts at the end of each lesson!

Traveling Waves

Sound and light both travel by waves. In order to hear sounds or see light, waves must travel from one place to another and enter either your ears or eyes. How do you think these waves travel? Circle the response that best matches your thinking.

A. One needs to travel through matter.

B. Neither needs to travel through matter.

C. They both need to travel through matter.

Explain your thinking. Describe your ideas about how sound and light waves move.

_____

_____

_____

_____

_____

_____

You will revisit your response to the Science Probe at the end of the lesson.

How Light Travels

ENCOUNTER
THE PHENOMENON
| How does light compare to sound?

GO ONLINE

Watch the video *Amazing Architecture* to see this phenomenon in action.

Imagine you are standing on a busy street looking up at the skyscrapers in the photo on the left. What would you hear? Record your thoughts in the box on the left. What do you see? Record your thoughts in the box on the right. Share your thoughts with a partner. Add any additional observations.

Sounds you hear	Sights you see

With your partner, discuss if sound and light have similarities to each other. Record your notes in the space below.

ENCOUNTER
THE PHENOMENON

When you look up at a skyscraper, you might see different materials such as brick, metal, and glass. You might see your reflection in a window or see through another window to the people inside the building. You might hear cars moving or people talking. How does light and what you see compare to sound and what you hear? Using your ideas about light and sound, make a claim about how light compares to sound.

CLAIM

Light is similar to and different from mechanical waves, like sound, by...

 COLLECT EVIDENCE as you work through the lesson.
Then return to these pages to record your evidence.

EVIDENCE

A. What evidence have you discovered to compare the properties of light and mechanical waves?

B. What evidence have you discovered to compare how light and sound travel through different mediums?

MORE EVIDENCE

C. What evidence have you discovered to compare how light and mechanical waves move away from a source?

When you are finished with the lesson, review your evidence. If necessary, based on the evidence, revise your claim.

REVISED CLAIM

Light is similar to and different from mechanical waves, like sound, by...

D. What evidence have you discovered to compare how light and mechanical waves interact with matter?

Finally, explain your reasoning for how and why your evidence supports your claim.

REASONING

The evidence I collected supports my claim because...

What is light?

Have you ever wondered what light is? Is it matter? Is it energy? Think about what makes up light. Record your notes in the first column. Pair with a partner and discuss his or her notes. Write any new notes in the second column. Then, record in the third column what you both would like to share about light with the class.

Think	Pair	Share

Light is neither matter nor energy. Light is a type of wave. **Light** is electromagnetic radiation that you can see. Electromagnetic radiation is a type of wave created by vibrating particles. These waves radiate, or spread out, electric and magnetic fields in all directions from a source. You might recall that waves carry energy. The energy carried by an electromagnetic wave is called **radiant energy.**

There are many different types of electromagnetic waves. These waves are classified by their wavelengths and frequencies in the electromagnetic spectrum, as shown below. The groups include radio waves, microwaves, infrared waves, ultraviolet waves, X-rays, and gamma rays along with light. Out of the entire electromagnetic spectrum, light is the only wave that you can see with your eyes.

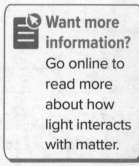

Want more information? Go online to read more about how light interacts with matter.

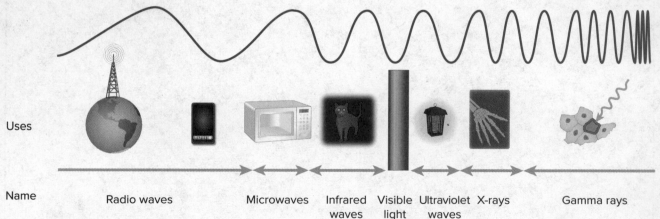

Uses

Name · Radio waves · Microwaves · Infrared waves · Visible light · Ultraviolet waves · X-rays · Gamma rays

What's the use?

If light is the only type of electromagnetic wave you can see, are the rest of the waves in the electromagnetic spectrum useful? Let's find out!

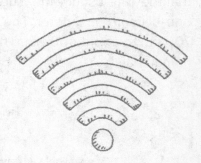

GO ONLINE Watch the animation *Electromagnetic Spectrum* to find out more about these waves. Then, complete the graphic organizer below.

Type	Describe the wave's wavelength, frequency, and energy	Example use or characteristic of the wave
Radio Waves		
Microwaves		
Infrared Waves		
Light		
Ultraviolet Waves		
X-rays		
Gamma Rays		

Properties of Light A light wave, just like a mechanical wave, has a wavelength and a frequency. The wavelengths of light waves are so short that they are usually measured in nanometers (nm). One nanometer equals one-billionth of a meter. The wavelengths of light waves range from about 700 nm to about 400 nm. This is about one-hundredth smaller than a human hair.

Orange light can have a wavelength between 590 nm and 620 nm and a frequency around 600 trillion Hz.

Energy The relationship between energy and other wave properties is different for mechanical waves and electromagnetic waves. The energy of a mechanical wave is related to its amplitude. A water wave, for example, with a high amplitude has a lot of energy. The energy of an electromagnetic wave is related to its frequency, not amplitude. As the frequency of an electromagnetic wave increases, the energy of the wave increases.

Brightness In astronomy, the amplitude of a light wave is related to the measured brightness of the light. The brightness of a light is a person's perception of intensity. Recall, intensity is the amount of energy that passes through a square meter of space in one second. Intensity depends on the amount of energy a source emits. Light from a flashlight, for example, has a much lower intensity than light from the Sun.

Intensity also depends on the light's distance from the source. When you're near a lamp, you probably notice that the intensity of the light is greater compared to when you're farther away from the lamp. Many of the stars in the top figure on the right emit as much energy as the Sun. However, the light from these stars is less intense than light from the Sun because the stars are farther away from Earth.

One person's eyes might be more sensitive to light than another person's eyes. As a result, different people might describe the intensity of a light differently. In addition, some eyes are more sensitive to some colors than others. The environment also can affect the brightness of a light. Many stars are visible in the top photo. Few stars are visible in the bottom photo because there are numerous light sources near the ground.

How does light reach Earth?

When you turn on a flashlight, light is produced. The flashlight is the source of the light. What is the source of light on Earth? You might say the Sun and you would be right. How does the light from the Sun reach Earth? Recall, mechanical waves, including sound, need a medium to travel through. Do electromagnetic waves also need a medium?

Read a Scientific Text

CLOSE READING

Inspect

Read the passage *Using the Electromagnetic Spectrum*.

Find Evidence

Reread the passage. Underline evidence on whether or not electromagnetic waves need a medium to travel through.

Make Connections

Communicate With your partner, construct an explanation on whether electromagnetic waves require a medium. Evaluate each other's explanations for solid evidence and reasoning.

Copyright © McGraw-Hill Education   (photo) NASA, ESA, R. O'Connell (University of Virginia), and the Hubble Heritage Team (STScI/AURA), (text)Vogt, Gregory L. Space-Based Astronomy: An Educator Guide with Activities for Science, Mathematics, and Technology Education. https://www.nasa.gov/pdf/319904main_The_Electromagnetic_ Spectrum.pdf

PRIMARY SOURCE

Using the Electromagnetic Spectrum

All objects in space are very distant and difficult for humans to visit. Only the Moon has been visited so far. Instead of visiting stars and planets, astronomers collect electromagnetic radiation from them using a variety of tools. Radio dishes capture radio signals from space. Big telescopes on Earth gather visible and infrared light. Interplanetary spacecraft have traveled to all the planets in our solar system except Pluto and have landed on two. No spacecraft has ever brought back planetary material for study. They send back all their information by radio waves.

Virtually everything astronomers have learned about the universe beyond Earth depends on the information contained in the electromagnetic radiation that has traveled to Earth. For example, when a star explodes as in a supernova, it emits energy in all wavelengths of the electromagnetic spectrum. The most famous supernova is the stellar explosion that became visible in 1054 and produced the Crab Nebula. [...]

Unfortunately for astronomical research, Earth's atmosphere acts as a filter to block most wavelengths in the electromagnetic spectrum. [...] Only small portions of the spectrum actually reach the surface. [...] More pieces of the puzzle are gathered by putting observatories at high altitudes (on mountain tops) where the air is thin and dry, and by flying instruments on planes and balloons. By far the best viewing location is outer space.

Source: National Aeronautics and Space Administration

EARTH SCIENCE **Connection** Recall that outer space is a vast emptiness with very few spots of matter in between. The space between matter is a vacuum. A vacuum is a volume of space that contains little or no matter. For sunlight or starlight to reach Earth, electromagnetic waves must travel through the vacuum of space. Because electromagnetic waves do not need matter to travel, they also do not create a disturbance in matter like mechanical waves do.

Speed of Light In a science fiction movie you may have heard, "We are moving at lightspeed!" What does "lightspeed" mean? Light, along with the other electromagnetic waves, travels through a vacuum at a speed of about 300,000 km/s. However, light waves slow down when they travel through matter. The speed of light in some different materials is listed in the table below. Light waves travel much faster than sound waves. For example, in air the speed of light is about 900,000 times faster than the speed of sound. This explains why you see lightning before you hear thunder.

Vista, CA

You will see lightning before hearing thunder because light travels faster than sound in the atmosphere.

Speed of Light Waves in Some Materials	
Material	Wave Speed (km/s)
Vacuum	300,000
Air	299,920
Water	225,100
Glass	193,000

THREE-DIMENSIONAL THINKING

What are some patterns, including similarities and differences, between electromagnetic waves, like light, and mechanical waves, like sound?

_____

_____

_____

_____

_____

COLLECT EVIDENCE

How do the mediums through which light and sound waves travel compare? Record your evidence (B) in the chart at the beginning of the lesson.

How does light move from a source to your eye?

Light is a type of electromagnetic wave and can move through a vacuum or a medium. Does light behave similarly to a water wave or a sound wave? How does it get from one point to the other? Let's find out!

 Lights out!

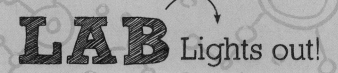

Safety

Materials

flashlight

fine-tooth comb

solid block

Procedure

1. Read and complete a lab safety form.

2. Turn on a flashlight. Shine it down onto a surface such as a desk or the floor. Describe the direction the light travels from the flashlight.

_____

_____

3. Set the flashlight on its side. Place the solid block 2–3 cm away from the flashlight. Describe what happens to the light when it hits the block.

_____

_____

4. Set the flashlight on its side. Place a fine-tooth comb 2–3 cm away from the flashlight. Describe the direction the light travels as it moves through the openings in the comb.

_____

_____

Analyze and Conclude

5. Draw a model of the light leaving the flashlight for A) when the flashlight is pointing down, B) when the block was in front of the flashlight, and C) when the comb was in front of the flashlight.

A	B	C

Light Sources To see an object there must be a source of light. An object that produces light is often described as emitting light. Examples of light sources include the Sun, traffic lights, and a firefly.

Light travels as waves moving away from a source. Scientists often describe these waves as countless numbers of light rays spreading out in all directions from a source. In the figure on the right you can see the shadows made by the tree trunks. The spaces between the rays are shadows or places with less light. The shadows show that light normally travels in a straight line. However, objects in the path of a light ray can cause the light ray to change direction. Light can also spread out slightly as it moves through a small opening.

THREE-DIMENSIONAL THINKING

Explain how you know light travels in straight lines and does not curve around objects. Support your explanation with evidence and reasoning.

_____

_____

_____

COLLECT EVIDENCE

How do light waves compare to how mechanical waves move away from a source? Record your evidence (C) in the chart at the beginning of the lesson.

How does light interact with matter?

Recall when a mechanical wave interacts with matter it can be transmitted, absorbed, or reflected. Do these interactions also happen to light waves? With a partner, develop a list of evidence you would need to support the claim that light waves can be transmitted, absorbed, or reflected. Record your supportive evidence in the table below.

San Francisco, CA

Evidence Needed For Light		
Transmission	Absorption	Reflection

 LAB Light and Matter

Safety

Materials

flashlight
beaker
mirror
note card

thermometer
water
empty milk jug
hole punch

Procedure

1. Read and complete a lab safety form.

2. Punch a hole in the note card. Place the note card over the flashlight to create a beam of light. This is your light ray.

3. Shine the light ray at the mirror from different directions. Record your observations in the Data and Observations section on the next page.

Copyright © McGraw-Hill Education (t)Nickolay Stanev/Shutterstock.com, (b)Studiohio/McGraw-Hill Education

Procedure, continued

4. Fill the beaker with water. Shine the light ray at the beaker. Record your observations.

5. Shine the light ray at the empty milk jug. Record your observations.

6. Shine the light ray at the bulb of a thermometer for about 1 min. Record your observations.

7. Follow your teacher's instructions for proper cleanup.

Data and Observations

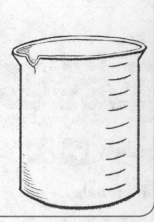

Analyze and Conclude

8. Did the evidence you collected support that light can be transmitted? Record your evidence and reasoning.

_____

_____

_____

_____

9. Did the evidence you collected support that light can be absorbed? Record your evidence and reasoning.

_____

_____

_____

_____

10. Did the evidence you collected support that light can be reflected? Record your evidence and reasoning.

_____

_____

_____

_____

Transmission Different types of matter interact with light in different ways. Air and clear glass transmit light with little or no distortion. A material that allows almost all of the light striking it to pass through, and through which objects can be seen clearly, is **transparent.** Examine the photo on the right. The squirrel is behind glass. It can be seen clearly because the glass is transparent. In the Lab *Light and Matter* the water and the glass beaker were also transparent.

Materials such as waxed paper or frosted glass also transmit light, but you cannot see through them clearly. A material that allows most of the light that strikes it to pass through, but through which objects appear blurry, is **translucent.** In the figure on the right, you cannot clearly see the two people talking behind the frosted glass because the glass is translucent. The milk jugs from the *Light and Matter* lab are also a translucent material.

Absorption Some materials absorb most of the light that strikes them. They transmit no light. Therefore, you cannot see objects through them. A material through which light does not pass is **opaque**. In the figure on the right the light-blocking curtains and the wooden frame are both opaque. You cannot see through them. You can only see through the transparent glass window panes.

Reflection When you look at a pane of glass, you sometimes can see an image of yourself. Light bounces off you, strikes the glass, and bounces back to your eye. Recall that the bouncing of a wave off a surface is called reflection. Reflected light allows an object to be seen.

Most types of matter interact with light in a combination of ways. For example, a window pane both transmits and reflects light. Some of the light that strikes an opaque object, such as a book, is absorbed and reflected at the same time.

THREE-DIMENSIONAL THINKING

A window's function is to allow you to see through into another space. Construct a model of the light rays that enable you to see an object through a window.

COLLECT EVIDENCE

How does light compare to how mechanical waves interact with different materials? Record your evidence (D) in the chart at the beginning of the lesson.

Light

◀ The lights used to keep this road safe contribute to light pollution.

This image was created using data gathered by satellites. It shows light pollution generated by human populations around the world.

Imagine trying to sleep in this house! Light shining in bedroom windows at night is a form of light pollution. ▶

Litter on the road, vehicle exhaust in the air, and fertilizer in a river's water are all types of pollution. But did you know that light also can be considered pollution? Light pollution is a problem in many urban areas worldwide.

Artificial lighting can be very useful. It can help keep areas free from crime and allow people to work and drive safely after dark. However, the lights people use often shine out into surrounding areas or up into the night sky. This is called light pollution.

Light pollution is a term that refers to the negative effects of artificial lighting. For example, light pollution can disrupt the daily cycles of nocturnal animals. Also, light that escapes into the atmosphere is wasted energy. In some areas, observing the night sky is very difficult because of light pollution.

Awareness of light pollution is increasing. Groups such as the American Medical Association (AMA) have recognized the negative impacts of light pollution. The AMA has passed resolutions advocating energy-efficient, fully shielded streetlight design. The structure of these lights are designed to reduce light pollution. Individuals can take steps to decrease light pollution by carefully choosing outdoor lights with light-pollution reduction in mind.

It's Your Turn

Observe and Draw Observe the night sky near your home, and make a drawing of what you observe. Then, discuss how light pollution in your area might compare with light pollution in other parts of the country.

Review

Summarize It!

1. **Restate** each term below in your own words. Use your classroom to find an example of each type of material, model light interaction in each system, and circle how light interacts with matter to produce the effect.

Type	Definition	Ray Model	Wave Interaction
Transparent			Reflected Transmitted Absorbed
Opaque			Reflected Transmitted Absorbed
Translucent			Reflected Transmitted Absorbed

Three-Dimensional Thinking

Use the model of the electromagnetic spectrum to answer question 2.

The Electromagnetic Spectrum

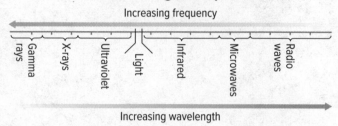

2. What pattern best describes the relationship between wavelength and frequency?

   A As frequency increases, wavelength increases.

   B As frequency decreases, wavelength decreases.

   C As frequency increases, wavelength decreases.

   D There is no relationship between wavelength and frequency.

Read the passage and then answer question 3.

> Stars and other objects in the universe give off, or emit, energy in the form of waves. Most stars emit energy in all wavelengths. But how much of each wavelength they emit depends on their temperatures. Hot stars emit mostly shorter waves with higher energy, such as X-rays, gamma rays, and ultraviolet waves. Cool stars emit mostly longer waves with lower energy, such as infrared waves and radio waves. The Sun has a medium temperature range. It emits much of its energy as visible light. These waves travel through vast regions of space and reach Earth.

3. Which argument is best supported by the passage?

   A The higher the temperature of a star, the more energy it emits.

   B Cool stars do not produce radio waves.

   C Visible light only comes from the Sun.

   D The amplitude of a light wave is determined by its energy.

Real-World Connection

4. **Model** You turn on a light in a dark room and see a chair. Sketch the path that the light waves travel to enable you to see the chair.

5. **Explain** You have been asked to help design a new media room. The criteria for the room includes shades that do not let in light from outside and are nonreflective. What properties should the material for the shades have?

_____

_____

_____

_____

 Still have questions?
Go online to check your understanding on how light interacts with matter.

REVISIT

PAGE KEELEY
SCIENCE PROBES

Do you still agree with the statement you chose at the beginning of the lesson? Return to the Science Probe at the beginning of the lesson. Explain why you agree or disagree with that statement now.

EXPLAIN
THE PHENOMENON

Revisit your claim on how light is similar to and different from mechanical waves, like sound. Review the evidence you collected. Explain how your evidence supports your claim.

START PLANNING

STEM Module Project Engineering Challenge

Now that you've learned about how light travels, go to your Module Project to examine some materials you might want to use in your optical illusion. Keep in mind how light interacts with transparent, translucent, and opaque materials.

Seeing a Flower

When we look at flowers, we see that they come in many different shapes, sizes, and colors. What happens between a flower and our eyes that enables us to see it? Circle the answer that best matches your thinking.

A. The light in the room lights up the flower so our eyes can see it.

B. Something goes from our eyes to the flower so we can see it.

C. Something goes from the flower to our eyes so we can see it.

D. Particles of color travel to our brain so we can see the flower.

E. Something goes back and forth between our eyes and the flower so we can see it.

Explain your thinking. Describe how it is possible for us to see the flower.

_____

_____

_____

_____

_____

_____

You will revisit your response to the Science Probe at the end of the lesson.

Reflection and Mirrors

ENCOUNTER
THE PHENOMENON
| Why are the African wild cat's eyes glowing?

GO ONLINE

Watch the video *Glowing Eyes* to see this phenomenon in action.

Record your observations from the video below.

Then, create a plan on how you can take a photograph of this phenomenon. Record your plan below.

EXPLAIN
THE PHENOMENON

You may have seen pictures of animals and people with glowing eyes. You may have seen a cat's eyes glow when a flashlight shines in its direction. What could make eyes glow in the dark? Using your ideas from the activity, make a claim about why eyes sometimes appear to glow in the dark.

CLAIM

Eyes sometimes appear to glow in the dark because...

 COLLECT EVIDENCE as you work through the lesson. Then return to these pages to record your evidence.

EVIDENCE

A. What evidence have you discovered to explain how light reflects off a plane mirror?

B. What evidence have you discovered to explain how light reflects off a curved mirror?

MORE EVIDENCE

C. What evidence have you discovered to explain what happens when light reflects off a rough surface?

When you are finished with the lesson, review your evidence. If necessary, based on the evidence, revise your claim.

REVISED CLAIM

Eyes sometimes appear to glow in the dark because...

Finally, explain your reasoning for how and why your evidence supports your claim.

REASONING

The evidence I collected supports my claim because...

What happens when light reflects off a smooth, flat surface?

Recall that light can reflect off surfaces. When light interacts with opaque objects, some of the light will bounce off. Think about how reflection of light allows you to look in a mirror. How does the light bounce off a shiny, flat object like a mirror? Let's investigate!

 **Mirrored View**

Safety

Materials

flashlight	mirror
white paper	metric ruler
black construction paper	protractor
hole punch	tape
modeling clay	

Procedure

1. Read and complete a lab safety form.

2. Punch a hole through the black construction paper and use tape to secure the paper over the flashlight.

3. Use the modeling clay to stand the mirror upright at one end of the white paper. Tilt the mirror so it leans slightly toward the table.

4. Find the center of the bottom edge of the mirror. Then, use the protractor and the metric ruler to draw a line down the middle of the white paper. This line should be perpendicular to the mirror. Label this line *N* for normal.

5. Draw lines on the white paper from the center mark at angles 30°, 45°, and 60° to line *N*.

6. Turn on the flashlight, point it at the mirror, and place it so the beam is along the 45° line. This is the angle of incidence. Have a partner draw a short line tracing the reflected light beam and mark the line *45*.

7. Repeat step 6 for the 30°, 60°, and *N* lines. Record your observations in the space below.

8. Remove the white paper from the setup. Measure and use the space below to record the angles that the reflected beams made with *N*.

9. Follow your teacher's instructions for proper cleanup.

Data and Observations

Analyze and Conclude

10. What patterns do you notice between the angles of incidence and the angles of the reflected light rays?

_____

_____

_____

Reflection of Light When you look at a pane of glass, you sometimes can see an image of yourself. Light bounces off you, strikes the glass, and bounces back to your eye. Think about a calm lake like the one on the right. You can see the reflection of the trees on the other side of the lake. This is how the mirror bounced the light in the Lab *Mirrored View.* Recall that the bouncing of a wave off a surface is called reflection.

 Yosemite Valley, CA

Suppose you toss a tennis ball against a wall. If you throw the ball straight toward the wall, it will bounce straight back to you. Where on the wall would you throw the ball so that a friend standing to your left could catch it? You might throw it toward a point on the wall halfway between you and your friend.

Law of Reflection Like the tennis ball, light behaves in predictable ways when it reflects. Recall that light moves in straight lines. These lines of light are represented in a model as straight arrows called rays. Scientists often use this model to trace the path of light. The rays in the ray diagram on the bottom right show how light reflects. An imaginary line perpendicular to a reflecting surface is called the normal. The light ray moving toward the surface is the incident ray. The light ray moving away is the reflected ray.

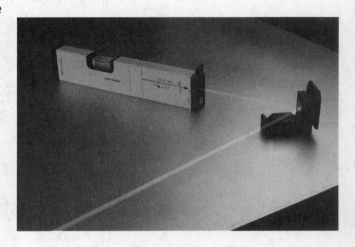

Notice the angle formed where an incident ray meets the normal. This is the angle of incidence. A reflected ray forms an identical angle on the other side of the normal. This angle is the angle of reflection. According to the **law of reflection,** when a wave is reflected from a surface, the angle of reflection is equal to the angle of incidence.

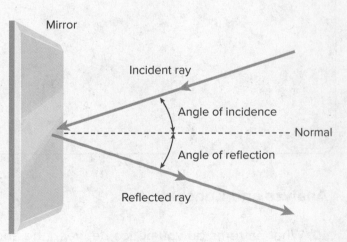

Mirror

Incident ray

Angle of incidence

Normal

Angle of reflection

Reflected ray

📋❌ Want more information?
Go online to read more about how light reflects off surfaces and mirrors.

FOLDABLES®
Go to the Foldables® library to make a Foldable® that will help you take notes while reading this lesson.

Images When you look into a mirror, it looks like you could touch the image in the mirror. When you look at ray diagrams, think about what you would see if the rays reflected into your eyes. Remember that your brain only perceives where the rays appear to come from, not their actual paths. Look at the figure to the right. The object is in front of the mirror, but you see the image of the object behind the mirror. A **virtual image** is an image of an object that your brain perceives to be in a place where the object is not. Objects seen in a plane, or flat, mirror are virtual images.

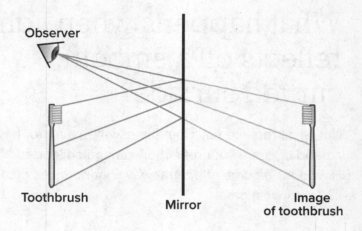

Observer

Toothbrush   Mirror   Image of toothbrush

GO ONLINE for more opportunities to explore!

Investigate how light moves and reflects by performing one of the following activities.

☐ **Design** a solution in the **Lab** *Back to Back*. **OR** ☐ **Model** light's paths in the **Investigation** *Plane Images*.

THREE-DIMENSIONAL THINKING
Label the rays and the angles in the **model** below. Indicate the location of the normal.

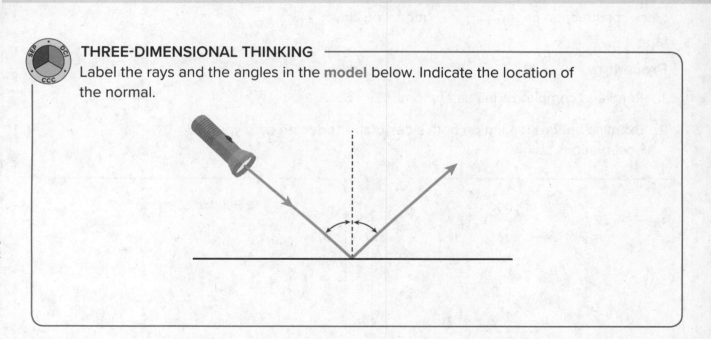

COLLECT EVIDENCE

How does the way light reflects off a plane mirror help explain why eyes sometimes appear to glow in the dark? Record your evidence (A) in the chart at the beginning of the lesson.

What happens when light reflects off a smooth, curved surface?

Not all mirrors are flat. Sometimes when a mirror has a bend or curve your reflection can look distorted. How does a curve affect the way light bounces off it? Let's investigate!

LAB Two Sided

Safety

Materials

flashlight

note card

black construction paper

tape

metal spoon

hole punch

modeling clay

Procedure

1. Read and complete a lab safety form.

2. Examine your reflection on both sides of the spoon. Record your observations below.

Inside of spoon	*Outside of spoon*

3. Punch a hole through the black construction paper and use tape to secure it over the flashlight.

4. Use the modeling clay to secure the spoon upright.

5. Shine the flashlight at the inner portion of the spoon.

6. Hold the note card near the spoon until you can see the light reflecting onto the note card.

7. Move the note card toward and away from the spoon. Record your observations below.

8. Turn the spoon around and shine the flashlight at the outer portion of the spoon. Repeat steps 5–6. Record your observations below.

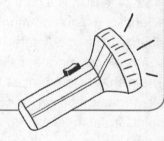

Analyze and Conclude

9. Which side of the spoon spread the light out in all directions?

10. Which side of the spoon focuses the light into a point?

Concave Mirrors Not all mirrors are flat. A mirror that curves inward is called a **concave mirror,** like the mirror in the figure below. A line perpendicular to the center of the mirror is the optical axis. The law of reflection determines the direction of reflected rays. When rays parallel to the optical axis strike a concave mirror, the reflected rays converge, or come together.

Focal Point Look again at the figure below. Notice the point where the rays converge. The point where light rays parallel to the optical axis converge after being reflected by a concave mirror is the **focal point.** Imagine that a concave mirror is part of a hollow sphere. The focal point is halfway between the mirror and the center of the sphere. The distance along the optical axis from the mirror to the focal point is the focal length. The lesser the curve of a mirror, the longer its focal length. The position of an object compared to the focal point determines the type of image formed by a concave mirror.

This explains how a satellite dish works. A satellite dish is a concave mirror that scientists use to communicate with objects in space. A satellite in orbit sends electromagnetic waves to Earth. The dish shape bounces the electromagnetic waves to the focal point. A sensor is placed at the focal point that receives the signal.

Convex Mirrors Have you ever seen a large, round mirror high in the corner of a hallway? The mirror enables someone to see places they cannot see with a plane mirror, and around corners where someone else may be walking. A mirror that curves outward, like the back of a spoon, is called a **convex mirror.** Light rays diverge, or spread apart, after they strike the surface of a convex mirror.

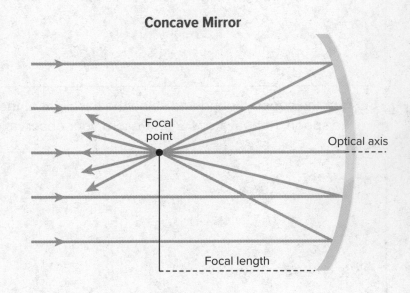

Concave Mirror

Focal point

Optical axis

Focal length

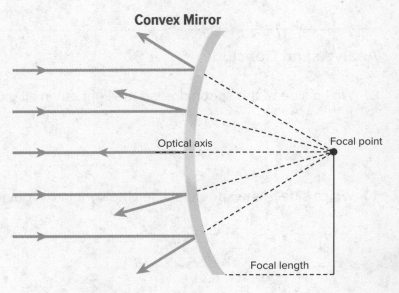

Convex Mirror

Optical axis

Focal point

Focal length

Types of Images As shown in the figure to the right, the image a concave mirror forms depends on the object's location relative to the focal point. The image is virtual if the object is between the focal point and the mirror. The image is real if the object is beyond the focal point. A **real image** is one that forms where rays converge. No image forms if the object is at the focal point.

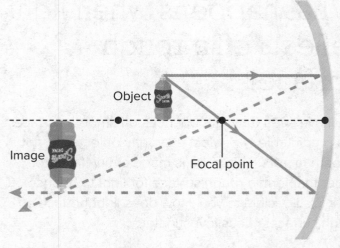

Object

Image

Focal point

THREE-DIMENSIONAL THINKING

Sketch a **model** of what happens to the light in a convex mirror.

How does the **structure** of convex mirrors support the **function** of side mirrors on cars?

_____

_____

_____

_____

_____

COLLECT EVIDENCE

How does the way light reflects off a curved mirror help explain why eyes sometimes appear to glow in the dark? Record your evidence (B) in the chart at the beginning of the lesson.

What happens when light reflects off a rough surface?

You have seen that light bounces off smooth surfaces in a predictable way. Most everyday objects are not smooth mirrors. This page is made of tiny fibers of paper that form a rough surface for light to bounce off, yet it is still visible to you. How does light bounce off rough surfaces? Let's investigate!

How do you see rough surfaces like the book?

LAB The Rough Side

Safety

Materials

flashlight

tape

modeling clay

black construction paper

hole punch

aluminum foil

Procedure

1. Read and complete a lab safety form.

2. Punch a hole through the black construction paper and use tape to secure it over the flashlight.

3. Crumple and straighten out the aluminum foil several times.

4. Push the aluminum foil into lumps of modeling clay so it stands vertically. Tilt the foil so it leans slightly toward the table.

5. Turn on the flashlight and place it so the beam is approximately at a 45° angle to the foil.

6. Record your observations in the Data and Observations section on the next page.

7. Follow your teacher's instructions for proper cleanup.

Data and Observations

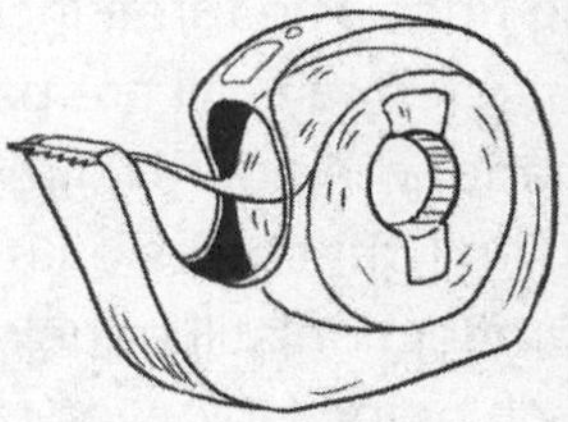

Analyze and Conclude

8. Sketch a model of the light reflecting off the aluminum foil. Include light rays before and after the reflection.

9. In what direction did the light reflect?

_____

_____

10. Does light reflect off a surface if there is no image formed? Explain.

_____

_____

_____

Regular and Diffuse Reflection You see objects when light reflects off them into your eyes. Why can you see your reflection in smooth, shiny surfaces but not in a piece of paper or a painted wall? The law of reflection applies whether the surface is smooth or rough. Reflection of light from a smooth, shiny surface is called **regular reflection.** Look at the figure to the right. The three incident rays and the three reflected rays all are parallel. You see a sharp image when parallel rays reflect into your eyes. When light strikes an uneven surface, the angle of reflection still equals the angle of incidence at each point. However, rays reflect in different directions. Reflection of light from a rough surface is called **diffuse reflection.**

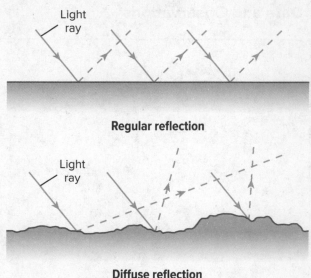

Regular reflection

Diffuse reflection

Scattering When a beam of sunlight shines through a window, you might notice tiny particles of dust. You see the dust particles because they reflect light waves. As the figure below shows, dust particles reflect light waves in many different directions because they have different shapes. This is an example of scattering.

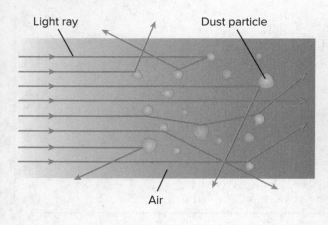

Big Sur, CA

Scattering occurs when light waves traveling in one direction are made to travel in many directions. The dust particles scatter the light waves in a sunbeam. If there are enough particles in the air, all of the light will be scattered. When this happens, no light will be transmitted. This is why clouds and fog are opaque. The water particles in the air reflect light. All the Sun's light is scattered, so the cloud appears opaque.

COLLECT EVIDENCE

How does the way light reflects off a rough surface help explain why eyes sometimes appear to glow in the dark? Record your evidence (C) in the chart at the beginning of the lesson.

A Closer Look: Retroreflectors

A retroreflector is a device that reflects light parallel to but in the opposite direction of the light source. The retroreflector can reflect light back to the source regardless of the angle of incidence. This means that the angle of incidence is 0°. It is possible to make retroreflectors as thin as a piece of paper.

Retroreflectors are used as safety equipment for objects that are difficult to see at night. The surface of roads have retroreflectors to reflect the light from a car's headlights back to the vehicle. This makes road markings able to be seen from all sides.

Retroreflectors have even been placed on the Moon for experiments. Scientists point lasers at the reflectors. The light bounces off the reflectors and travels back to the scientists' laboratories. The scientists can measure how long it takes for the light to travel to the Moon and back. Knowing how long it takes for light to travel, the distance can be calculated with high precision. This is how we know the Moon is drifting away from Earth at a rate of about 4 cm a year.

A retroreflector on the Moon.

It's Your Turn

Research Retroreflectors are used for many scientific purposes and safety technology. Research one way that a retroreflective surface is used today, and make a presentation about the surface and its uses.

Review

Summarize It!

1. **Illustrate** Draw the path of light from a light source to the eye. Then complete the sequence diagram to explain what you have drawn.

Eye

Sun

Object

| Light source emits _____ | | Light rays _____ off an object. | | Light rays reflected off an object _____ |

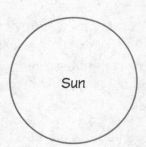

Three-Dimensional Thinking

Use the model below to answer questions 2 and 3.

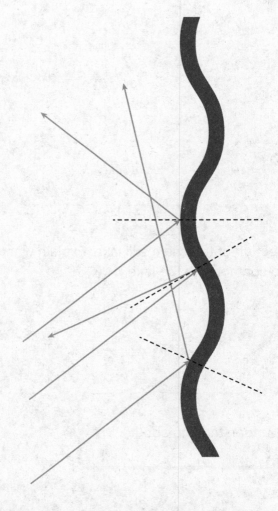

2. Which object has a surface structure that reflects light rays in the functional manner shown in the model above?

   A convex mirror

   B glass window

   C polished silver spoon

   D pond with ripples

3. What type of reflection is modeled?

   A diffuse reflection

   B real image

   C virtual image

   D regular reflection

Real-World Connection

4. **Explain** When you turn on a lamp, you are able to see everything in a room. Explain why you see the lamp. Then, explain why you see other objects in the room.

_____

_____

_____

_____

_____

5. **Describe** You see the reflection of trees in a still lake. Explain what happens to the light as it comes into contact with the lake.

_____

_____

_____

 Still have questions?
Go online to check your understanding about reflection and mirrors.

 **REVISIT**
PAGE KEELEY SCIENCE PROBES
Do you still agree with the statement you chose at the beginning of the lesson? Return to the Science Probe at the beginning of the lesson. Explain why you agree or disagree with that statement now.

EXPLAIN
THE PHENOMENON

Revisit your claim about how eyes sometimes seem to glow in the dark. Review the evidence you collected. Explain how your evidence supports your claim.

KEEP PLANNING
STEM Module Project Engineering Challenge

Now that you've learned about reflection and mirrors, go back to your Module Project to explain different ideas of how to make reflection the center of an optical illusion. Keep in mind how light reflects to make images appear different than they actually are.

Through the Lens

A camera lens can make an image larger or smaller. How does a lens affect the size of an image? Circle the answer that best matches your thinking.

A. When a lens is moved back and forth, an image will become bigger or smaller but will always remain sharp.

B. The shape of the lens does not matter because light always passes straight through transparent objects.

C. The size of the image depends on the diameter of the lens.

D. The size of the image depends on the shape of the lens.

Explain your thinking. Describe your ideas about how a lens affects an image.

_____

_____

_____

_____

_____

_____

You will revisit your response to the Science Probe at the end of the lesson.

Refraction and Lenses

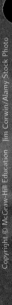

ENCOUNTER
THE PHENOMENON | Why does the polar bear's body look different in the water?

Your teacher will provide you with some pieces of shaped glass. Use the glass to find other ways that light can interact with matter. Draw what you see.

Light and Water

▶

GO ONLINE
Watch the video *Light and Water* to see this phenomenon in action.

EXPLAIN
THE PHENOMENON

You may have noticed that a drinking straw appears to bend in a glass of water. You may have also noticed that lenses can make objects appear larger or smaller. These phenomena are related. What makes the polar bear's body look different in the water? Make a claim about what changes the polar bear's appearance in the water.

CLAIM

The polar bear's body looks different in the water because...

 COLLECT EVIDENCE as you work through the lesson. Then return to these pages to record your evidence.

EVIDENCE

A. What evidence have you discovered to explain what happens when light passes through different mediums?

MORE EVIDENCE

B. What evidence have you discovered to explain how lenses affect the way an image is seen?

When you are finished with the lesson, review your evidence. If necessary, based on the evidence, revise your claim.

REVISED CLAIM

The polar bear's body looks different in the water because...

Finally, explain your reasoning for how and why your evidence supports your claim.

REASONING

The evidence I collected supports my claim because...

What happens when light passes through a medium other than air?

Think about swimming in a pool. Have you ever noticed that the light at the bottom of the pool makes patterns based on how the water is moving? Light is transmitted through the water. Does the light bend with the water? Let's investigate!

Want more information?
Go online to read more about how light refracts in materials.

FOLDABLES
Go to the Foldables® library to make a Foldable® that will help you take notes while reading this lesson.

LAB Bending Light

Safety

Materials

water	large beaker
coin	wooden skewer

Procedure

1. Read and complete a lab safety form.

2. Fill a large beaker with water.

3. Hold a coin on one side of the beaker and observe the coin through the water. Record your observations in the space below.

4. Place the coin in the beaker of water. Observe the coin from above.

5. With your wooden skewer, try to touch the coin from above. Record your observations in the Data and Observations section on the next page.

Copyright © McGraw-Hill Education (t)Jingram Publishing, (b)maogg/iStock/Getty Images

6. Follow your teacher's instructions for proper cleanup.

Data and Observations

Analyze and Conclude

7. What adjustments to your aim did you make to touch the coin in the beaker?

_____

_____

8. Model what you think is happening to the transmitted light wave as it moves from the coin to your eye.

9. Imagine you had a laser pointer. Where would you aim to put the laser on the coin? Explain.

_____

_____

_____

Medium Interactions Have you ever tried to pick up something from the bottom of a container of water and the object was deeper than you thought it was? This happens because when light waves are transmitted, they can change direction. Light always travels through empty space at the same speed, 300,000 km/s. Light travels more slowly through a medium, such as air, glass, or water. The particles of the material interact with the light waves and slow them down. Some substances, such as air, only slow light a small amount. Others, such as glass, slow the light more.

Refraction of Light Because the speed of light changes as it transmits from one medium to another, the direction of the light will change. If light enters the new medium at an angle, the wave will change direction. The change in direction of a wave as it changes speed while moving from one medium to another is called **refraction.** For example, when you visit an aquarium, the light bounces off the fish and to your eye. However, when the light is transmitted from the water to the air, it changes direction. You always see the fish further away than the fish actually is. This means, unless the fish is out of water, you can only see a virtual image of the fish.

Monterey Bay Aquarium, CA

Index of Refraction Each transparent material has a property called the index of refraction, as shown in the table. A medium that has a high index of refraction is sometimes called "slow" because light moves more slowly through it. A medium that has a relatively low index of refraction, such as air, is called "fast." When light is transmitted between two materials, the angle light refracts is dependent on the difference between the indices of refraction of the two objects. If the index of refraction is the same, the light will not refract.

Material	Index of Refraction	Wave Speed (km/s)
Vacuum	1.0000	300,000
Air	1.0003	299,920
Water	1.333	225,100
Glass	1.55	193,000

Slower Mediums Suppose you roll a toy car across a table straight at a piece of fabric. The front tires of the car slow down when they hit the fabric. The car continues to move in a straight line but more slowly. If you roll the car at an angle, one of the front tires will hit the fabric before the other. That side of the car will slow down, but the rest of the car will continue at the same speed until the other tire hits the fabric. This will cause the car to turn and change direction. A light wave behaves in a similar way when it moves into a slower medium, as shown in the figure. Recall that the normal is a line perpendicular to a surface. As light moves into a slower medium at an angle, it changes direction toward the normal.

Faster Mediums What happens when light in the figure moves back into the air? Suppose you ride your bike from a sidewalk into a muddy field and then back onto a sidewalk. You use the same energy to pedal the whole time, but you move more slowly in the mud. When you move back onto the sidewalk, you speed up. Similarly, as light moves into a medium with a lower index of refraction, it speeds up. The wave is still at an angle, so the part that leaves the slower medium first speeds up sooner. This causes the wave to turn away from the normal.

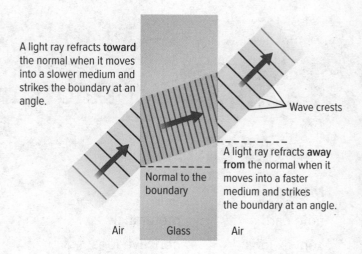

A light ray refracts **toward** the normal when it moves into a slower medium and strikes the boundary at an angle.

Wave crests

Normal to the boundary

A light ray refracts **away from** the normal when it moves into a faster medium and strikes the boundary at an angle.

Air   Glass   Air

THREE-DIMENSIONAL THINKING

The light from the Sun travels through a vacuum to Earth's atmosphere. Make an **argument from evidence** that the Sun actually goes below the horizon before you see it set in the west.

COLLECT EVIDENCE

How does light passing through different mediums help explain why the polar bear looks different in the water? Record your evidence (A) in the chart at the beginning of the lesson.

How do lenses affect how an image is seen?

Light changes direction as it passes through a medium. One medium that is used to change the direction of light is a lens. Lenses can be found in eyeglasses, cameras, telescopes, and binoculars. How does the shape of the lens and the distance of the lens from the object affect the image you see? Let's investigate!

LAB Looking Through Lenses

Safety

Materials

note card	meterstick
convex lens	concave lens
book	

Procedure

1. Read and complete a lab safety form.

2. Prop a book upright. Hold a convex lens at arm's length and 1.5 m from the book. Look at the book through the lens. Record your observations in the space below.

3. Slowly walk toward the book, keeping the lens at arm's length. Have your partner measure the distance from the lens to the book whenever the image changes significantly. Record your data and observations in the space below.

4. With the classroom lights dimmed, hold a note card in front of a window. Hold the lens between the note card and the window.

5. Try to focus an image of the scene outside onto the note card by moving the card closer and farther from the lens. When the image is focused as clearly as possible, have your partner measure the distance between the lens and the note card. Record your data and observations below.

6. Repeat steps 2–5 with a concave lens. Record your data and observations.

7. Follow your teacher's instructions for proper cleanup.

Analyze and Conclude

8. Identify positions of each lens when you saw significant changes in the image. What do you think caused these?

Lenses Binoculars, eyeglasses, your eyes, and cameras contain lenses. A **lens** is a transparent object with at least one curved side that causes light to change direction. Recall that most of the light that strikes a transparent material passes through it. Light refracts as it passes through a lens. The greater the curve of the lens, the more the light refracts. The direction of refraction depends on whether the lens is curved outward or inward.

In the figure below, light beams pass through two different lenses from the right. A lens that is thicker in the middle than at the edges is a **convex lens.** Notice that the light rays that move through a convex lens come together, or converge. A lens that is thicker at the edges than in the middle is a **concave lens.** Notice that the light rays spread apart, or diverge, as they move through a concave lens.

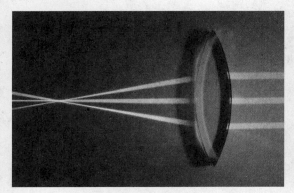

Convex Lens

Concave Lens

Convex Lenses The refraction of light by a convex lens is shown in the figure to the right. Notice that the normal to the curved surface slants toward the optical axis. Recall that light moving into a slower medium turns toward the normal. As a result, a convex lens refracts light inward and it converges.

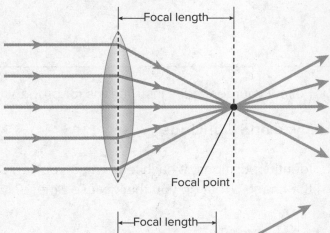

Focal length

Focal point

Concave Lenses Light rays that pass through a concave lens diverge, or spread apart. The figure on the bottom right shows why. Notice that the normal to the curved surface slants away from the optical axis. A line perpendicular to the center of the lens is the optical axis. Because light entering a slower medium changes direction toward the normal, the lens refracts light outward, or diverges.

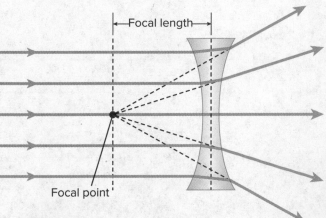

Focal length

Focal point

LIFE SCIENCE ▶ Connection Human eyes contain lenses, as well as other tissues, that can enable a person to see. The structure of a human eye is shown below. To see an object, light waves from an object travel through two convex lenses in the eye. Light waves first travel through the cornea (KOR nee uh), as shown below. The cornea is a convex lens made of transparent tissue located on the outside of the eye. Most of the change in direction of light rays occurs at the cornea.

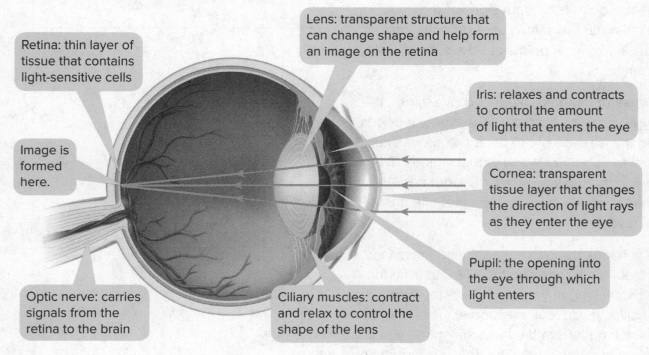

Retina: thin layer of tissue that contains light-sensitive cells

Lens: transparent structure that can change shape and help form an image on the retina

Iris: relaxes and contracts to control the amount of light that enters the eye

Image is formed here.

Cornea: transparent tissue layer that changes the direction of light rays as they enter the eye

Optic nerve: carries signals from the retina to the brain

Ciliary muscles: contract and relax to control the shape of the lens

Pupil: the opening into the eye through which light enters

Next the light travels through the iris to the second lens, which is simply called the lens. It is made of flexible, transparent tissue. The lens enables the eye to form a sharp image of nearby and distant objects. The muscles surrounding the lens change the lens's shape. To focus on nearby objects, these muscles relax and the lens becomes more curved.

To focus on distant objects, these muscles pull on the lens and make it flatter. The image created by the light passing through these lenses is then projected on a thin layer of tissue at the back of the eye. Special cells in this layer convert the image into electrical signals. Nerves carry these signals to the brain.

Some vision problems are caused by the cornea's structure. When the cornea fails to form an image on the back of the eye, corrective lenses can be worn to direct the light. Each lens has a particular structure and function that depends on the vision problem. Some lenses diverge the light because the cornea is overly curved. Other lenses converge the light because the cornea is too flat.

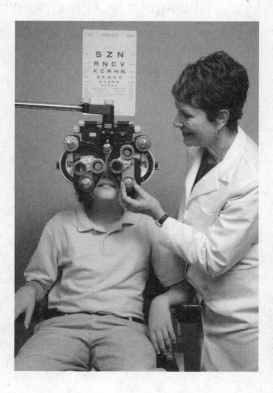

Focal Point and Focal Length Similar to a mirror, the point where rays parallel to the optical axis converge after passing through a lens is the focal point. The distance along the optical axis between the lens and the focal point is the focal length of the lens. Because you can look through a lens from either side, a focal point is on both sides of the lens. For a lens with the same curve on both sides, the lens's two focal points are the same distance from it.

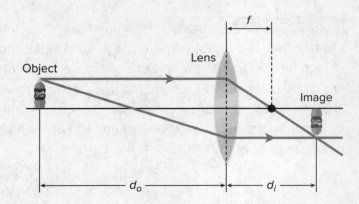

Types of Images Like a concave mirror, the type of image a convex lens forms depends on the location of the object. A convex lens can form both real and virtual images. The diagrams show only two rays, but remember that in reality, there are an indefinite number of rays.

If you look through a magnifying lens at an object more than one focal length from the lens, the image you see is inverted and smaller. If you look at an object less than one focal length from the lens, the image you see is upright and larger. The image is virtual because your brain interprets the rays as moving in a straight line.

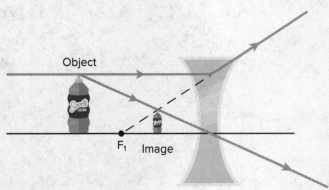

THREE-DIMENSIONAL THINKING

Starlight comes from so far away that it comes to Earth in parallel waves. Make a **model** of this light, and a lens that you would use to collect light at the end of a telescope.

COLLECT EVIDENCE

How does the way images are seen through a lens help explain why the polar bear looks different in the water? Record your evidence (B) in the chart at the beginning of the lesson.

A Closer Look: Fresnel Lens

Pescadero, CA

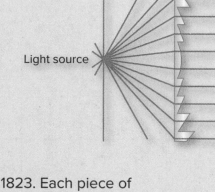

Sailing the seas can be dangerous even with modern technology. Imagine being a sailor that transports goods across the ocean in the 17th century. You navigate by stars and sail bravely towards shore. Before you can even see the lighthouse, you have already hit land.

Lighthouses in the 17th century had oil lamps that were difficult to see even when sailors were close to shore. The light from the flame spread out and dispersed in all directions. In an attempt to produce more light, lighthouse designers placed reflectors behind the flame. However, experiments showed that even the highest quality reflectors only sent about 39% of the light in a useful direction.

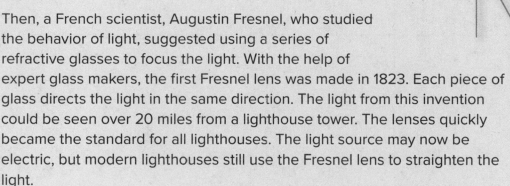

Fresnel lens

Light source

Then, a French scientist, Augustin Fresnel, who studied the behavior of light, suggested using a series of refractive glasses to focus the light. With the help of expert glass makers, the first Fresnel lens was made in 1823. Each piece of glass directs the light in the same direction. The light from this invention could be seen over 20 miles from a lighthouse tower. The lenses quickly became the standard for all lighthouses. The light source may now be electric, but modern lighthouses still use the Fresnel lens to straighten the light.

It's Your Turn

Research Fresnel lenses are useful for many functions because the lenses' structure can be much thinner than standard glass lenses. Research ways that a Fresnel lens is used in modern technology. Create a presentation on your findings and share with your class.

Review

Summarize It!

1. **Categorize** Complete the table by describing each type of lens.

Lens	Direction of Curvature	Direction of Refracted Light	System Model
Concave			
Convex			

Three-Dimensional Thinking

Use the model below to answer question 2.

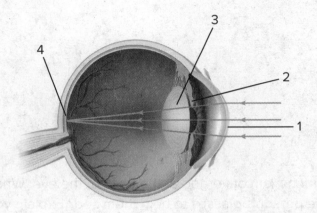

2. Which part of the eye can change its structure as a function to form a focused image?

   A 1

   B 2

   C 3

   D 4

---

3. Which of the following arguments identifies the best explanation about a concave lens being used to start a fire?

   A A concave lens will focus the Sun's light into a point that will cause a piece of paper to catch on fire.

   B Because the Sun's light comes from all directions, a concave lens will straighten the light onto the paper causing the paper to catch on fire.

   C Because a concave lens diverges the light, the Sun's light will not focus on the paper and no fire will occur.

   D `A concave lens will focus the Sun's light before the light can reach the paper, and no fire will occur.

Real-World Connection

4. Infer Suppose the light converged before reaching the back of the eye. What lenses would be in the person's glasses to help them see? Explain your choice.

_____

_____

_____

_____

5. Infer Suppose the light never converged at the back of the eye. What lenses would be in the person's glasses to help them see? Explain your choice.

_____

_____

_____

_____

 Still have questions?
Go online to check your understanding about refraction and lenses.

REVISIT SCIENCE PROBES

Do you still agree with the statement you chose at the beginning of the lesson? Return to the Science Probe at the beginning of the lesson. Explain why you agree or disagree with that statement now.

EXPLAIN THE PHENOMENON

Revisit your claim about why the appearance of the polar bear changed through the water. Review the evidence you collected. Explain how your evidence supports your claim.

KEEP PLANING

STEM Module Project Engineering Challenge

Now that you've learned about refraction and lenses, go back to your Module Project to show different ideas of how to make refraction the center of an optical illusion. Keep in mind how light refracts to make images appear different than they actually are.

Crayon Color

When you look around, there are many beautiful colors everywhere—reds, yellows, browns, blues. Why are you able to see that a blue crayon is blue?

A. Blue is a property of the crayon.

B. White light illuminates the blue crayon.

C. Blue light is reflected off the crayon.

D. The crayon is absorbing blue light.

Explain your thinking. Describe your ideas about how the different colors are seen.

_____

_____

_____

_____

_____

_____

_____

You will revisit your response to the Science Probe at the end of the lesson.

Color of Light

ENCOUNTER
THE PHENOMENON | How do colors appear from white light?

🔘 **GO ONLINE**

Watch the video *Sparkling Stones* to see this phenomenon in action.

Your teacher will provide you with a CD. Examine the blank side of the CD. Record what happens when you tilt the CD back and forth.

Once you have recorded your observations, obtain a flashlight and a piece of white paper. Set the piece of paper against a wall or an upright book. Your teacher will turn off the lights in the classroom. Aim the flashlight at the CD. See if you can get an image to form on the paper. Record your observations.

ENCOUNTER
THE PHENOMENON

Have you ever seen colors of light dancing around a room? When you look for the source, you might see that light is being refracted through a cut glass surface. Why doesn't this happen when light passes through a window? Where are the colors coming from? Using your observations from the flashlight and the CD activity, make a claim about why colors appear from white light.

CLAIM

Colors appear from white light because...

COLLECT EVIDENCE as you work through the lesson. Then return to these pages to record your evidence.

EVIDENCE

A. What evidence have you discovered to explain the colors of light?

MORE EVIDENCE

B. What evidence have you discovered to explain how different colors of light affect how you see color?

When you are finished with the lesson, review your evidence. If necessary, based on the evidence, revise your claim.

REVISED CLAIM

Colors appear from white light because...

Finally, explain your reasoning for how and why your evidence supports your claim.

REASONING

The evidence I collected supports my claim because...

Why are there different colors of light?

You know that light is a type of wave. It can be absorbed, transmitted, reflected, and refracted. What happened to the light when it hit the CD? You might have seen different colors form. When you shine white light through a prism, you also see different colors when the light exits the prism, from the other side. Does a prism use wave interactions of matter to form different colors? Let's investigate!

 Want more information?
Go online to read more about colors of light.

FOLDABLES
Go to the Foldables® library to make a Foldable® that will help you take notes while reading this lesson.

LAB Rainbow Bright

Safety

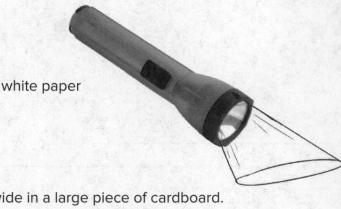

Materials

cardboard   scissors   white paper

prism   flashlight

Procedure

1. Read and complete a lab safety form.

2. Cut a slit about 3 cm long and 0.5 cm wide in a large piece of cardboard.

3. Hold the cardboard in a sunny window so the sunlight shines through the slit. In your other hand, hold a prism in front of the cardboard so the sunlight passes through it. Have another group member hold a sheet of white paper. Move or rotate the prism until the light shining through it falls on the paper. Describe and draw what you observe.

4. Shine the flashlight through the slit in the cardboard and then through the prism on to the white paper. Describe and draw what you observe.

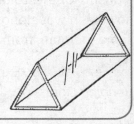

5. Follow your teacher's instructions for proper cleanup.

Analyze and Conclude

6. What causes the sunlight to change as it passes through the prism?

_____

_____

7. Did you observe the same effect with the flashlight as with the sunlight? Why or why not?

_____

_____

Light and Color Light that you see as white is actually a combination of light waves of many different wavelengths. When the white light refracts through a prism, you see different colors of light. The colors you may see include red, orange, yellow, green, blue, indigo, and violet. Each name represents a family of colors, each with a range of wavelengths. For instance, red light has a wavelength that varies from 780 nm to 622 nm and the wavelength of blue light varies from 492 nm to 455 nm.

Some lights, such as stage and neon lights, emit colored light. The color of an object that emits light depends on the wavelengths of the light given off. For example, a red neon light emits mostly red wavelengths along with some orange, yellow, and green wavelengths. It does not emit all of the wavelengths that the Sun emits.

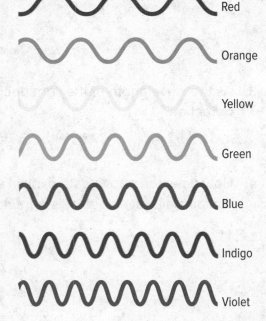

Color Differences

Light has to be refracted though a medium, such as a prism, for the colors to spread out. Let's investigate how each wavelength of light refracts though the same medium, from air to glass.

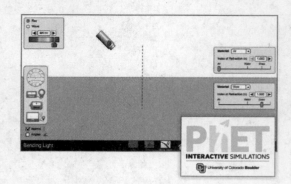

▶ **GO ONLINE**   Explore the PhET interactive simulation *Bending Light*.

After exploring the simulation on your own, reset the simulation and follow the instructions.

1. Go to the "More Tools" page. Turn on the angles. Complete the table below for each requested wavelength.

Wavelength (nm)	Color	Angle of Refraction	Speed of Light in Air (c)	Speed of Light in Glass (c)	Index of Refraction (Glass)
650					
615					
580					
530					
490					
460					
410					

2. Identify any patterns in the data.

_____

_____

3. As the wavelength of the light decreased, what happened to the angle of refraction?

_____

_____

4. How does the above data explain what happens when white light, that contains all wavelengths, is refracted through a glass prism?

_____

_____

_____

Separating Colors of Light In the Lab *Rainbow Bright* you learned that white light is made up of different colors. Recall that each color has a different wavelength and frequency. Waves with longer wavelengths and higher frequencies travel at greater speeds in a medium than waves with shorter wavelengths and lower frequencies. Therefore, when entering a medium, light with lower frequencies travels faster and refracts less than light with higher frequencies. Violet wavelengths refract the most because their frequencies are the highest. Red wavelengths have the lowest frequencies and refract the least. This causes the colors of light to spread out when they are refracted though a prism.

Read a Scientific Text

Copyright © McGraw-Hill Education   (Photo)Charlie Edward/iStockphoto/Getty Images, (Text) Newton, Isaac. Opticks: or a treatise of the reflections, refractions & colours of light. London: 1730.

HISTORY ⟩ Connection   One of the first people to record notes on the refraction of white light was Sir Isaac Newton. In 1704, Newton published *Opticks: or, A Treatise of the Reflexions, Refractions, Inflexions and Colours of Light.* Read an excerpt from the published work below.

CLOSE READING

Inspect
Read the passage *Opticks*.

Find Evidence
Reread the passage. Underline the observable evidence that Newton saw to indicate different colors of light refract at different angles.

Make Connections
Communicate With your partner, discuss how Newton determined which end of the color spectrum refracted more. Support your decision with the evidence you collected.

PRIMARY SOURCE

Opticks

I held it and the prism before a window in such manner that the sides of the paper were parallel to the prism, and both those sides and the prism were parallel to the horizon, and the cross line was also parallel to it: and that the light which fell from the window upon the paper made an angle with the paper, equal to that angle which was made with the same paper by the light reflected from it to the eye. Beyond the prism was the wall of the chamber under the window covered over with black cloth, and the cloth was involved in darkness that no light might be reflected from thence, which in passing by the edges of the paper to the eye, might mingle itself with the light of the paper, and obscure the phenomenon thereof. These things being thus ordered, I found that if the refracting angle of the prism be turned upwards, so that the paper may seem to be lifted upwards by the refraction, its blue half will be lifted higher by the refraction than its red half. But if the refracting angle of the prism be turned downward, so that the paper may seem to be carried lower by the refraction, its blue half will be carried something lower thereby than its red half. Wherefore in both cases the light which comes from the blue half of the paper through the prism to the eye, does in like circumstances suffer a greater refraction than the light which comes from the red half, and by consequence [refracts more].

Source: Opticks: or, A Treatise of the Reflexions, Refractions, Inflexions and Colours of Light

EARTH SCIENCE ▸ **Connection** You may have noticed that when a prism refracts the colors of light, they appear in the same order as in a rainbow. Do rainbows in nature come from a prism? You may have seen a rainbow appear in the sky during or after a rain shower. Rainbows form when water droplets in the air function like prisms and refract light. Each wavelength of light refracts as it enters the droplet, reflects back into the droplet, and refracts again when it leaves the droplet. Notice in the figure below that wavelengths of light near the blue end of the spectrum refract more than wavelengths near the red end of the spectrum. This effect produces the separate colors you see in a rainbow.

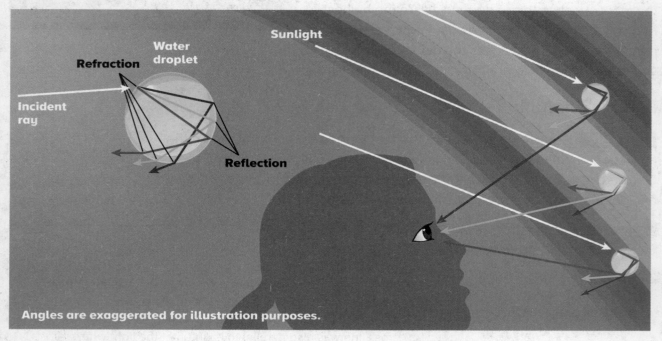

Angles are exaggerated for illustration purposes.

THREE-DIMENSIONAL THINKING

WRITING ▸ **Connection** Construct an **argument** to explain whether or not you would see a rainbow if your eyes only detected one wavelength of light.

_____

_____

_____

_____

_____

_____

LIFE SCIENCE Connection Recall that light is the only part of the electromagnetic spectrum that the human eye can see. You have learned when light enters the eye it is refracted through the cornea and the lens to form an image on the back of your eye. This part of your eye is called the retina. The retina is a layer of special light-sensitive cells in the back of the eye, as shown in the figure below. There, chemical reactions produce nerve signals that the optic nerve sends to your brain. There are two types of light-sensitive cells in your retina—rod cells and cone cells.

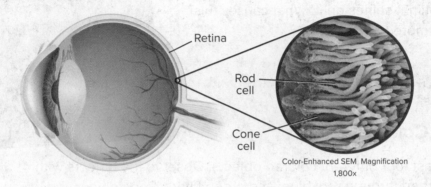

Retina

Rod cell

Cone cell

Color-Enhanced SEM Magnification 1,800x

Rod Cells There are more than 100 million rod cells in a human retina. Rod cells are sensitive to low light levels. They enable people to see objects in dim light. However, the signals rod cells send to your brain do not enable you to see colors.

Cone Cells A retina contains over 6 million cone cells. Cone cells enable a person to see colors. However, cone cells need brighter light than rod cells to function. In very dim light, only rod cells function. That is why objects seem to have no color in very dim light. The responses of cone cells to light waves with different wavelengths enable you to see different colors.

The retina has three types of cone cells. Each type of cone cell responds to a different range of wavelengths. This means that different wavelengths of light cause each type of cone cell to send different signals to the brain. Your brain interprets the different combinations of signals from the three types of cone cells as different colors. However, in some people not all three types of cone cells function properly. These people cannot detect certain colors. This condition is commonly known as color blindness, but is more appropriately called color deficiency. People with some kinds of color deficiency cannot see the number 74 in the figure to the right.

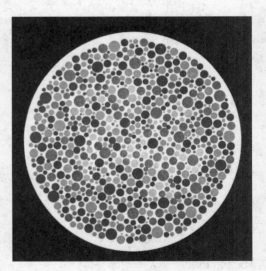

COLLECT EVIDENCE

How do the properties of each color of light explain how they appear from white light? Record your evidence (A) in the chart at the beginning of the lesson.

How do different colors of light affect what we see?

You may have noticed at a concert that the colors of objects on stage depend on the colors of the spotlights. A shirt that appears blue when a white spotlight shines on it may appear black when a red spotlight shines on it. That same shirt will appear blue when a blue spotlight shines on it. What causes this? Let's investigate more to find out!

How does a red filter change the colors that you see?

INVESTIGATION

Concepts of Color

1. Choose at least four different colored objects. Observe the objects with no filter and then through red, blue, and green filters. Record your observations in the space below.

View	Observations
No Filter	Object 1: Object 2: Object 3: Object 4:
Red Filter	Object 1: Object 2: Object 3: Object 4:
Blue Filter	Object 1: Object 2: Object 3: Object 4:
Green Filter	Object 1: Object 2: Object 3: Object 4:

2. Contrast your observations with and without filters.

_____

_____

_____

3. Explain why you think the objects you observed appeared to change color when you used a filter.

_____

_____

_____

4. Working with two other people, have each person place one of the filters over his or her flashlight. Turn on the flashlight and aim all three flashlights at a sheet of white paper attached to the wall. Adjust the beams until you can see three circles that overlap. Each color should overlap both of the other colors, and all three colors should overlap in the middle. Use crayons or colored markers to draw what you see in the space below.

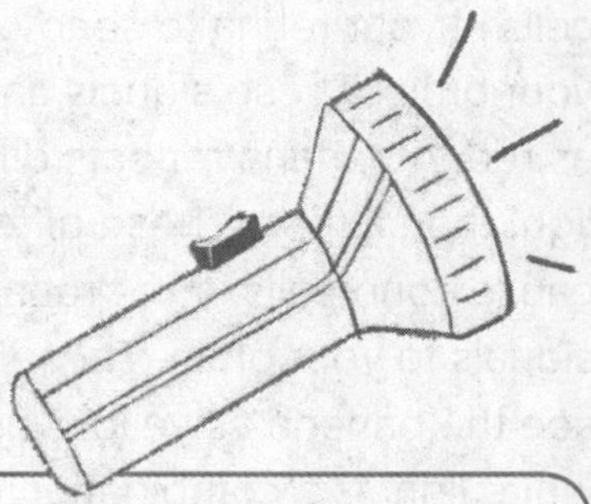

5. Explain why you think the eye sees different colors on different parts of the paper.

_____

_____

_____

Color of Objects The objects you see around you are different colors. A banana is mostly yellow, but a rose might be red. Why is a banana a different color than a rose? Bananas and roses do not give off, or emit, light.

When light waves of different wavelengths interact with an object, the object absorbs some light waves and reflects others. The wavelengths of light waves absorbed and reflected are determined by the particles that make up the object. Different particles absorb different wavelengths of light.

For example, the figure on the right shows that the rose is red because the petals of the rose reflect light waves with certain wavelengths. When these light waves enter your eye, they cause the cone cells in your retina to send certain nerve signals to your brain. These signals cause you to see the rose as red. A banana reflects different wavelengths of light than a rose. These different wavelengths cause cone cells in the retina to send different signals to your brain. These signals cause you to see the banana as yellow instead of red. Recall that white light is a combination of all the wavelengths of light. To see a white object, all light wavelengths are reflected. A black object absorbs all wavelengths of light and there is no reflected light. Your brain interprets the absence of light as the color black.

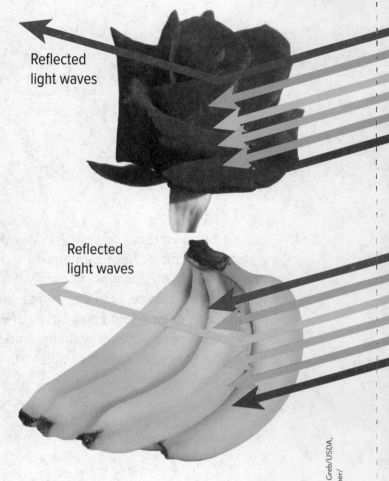

Reflected light waves

Reflected light waves

You may think that light waves have colors. Color, however, is a sensation produced by your brain when light waves enter your eyes. Light waves have no color as they travel from an object to your eyes.

EARTH SCIENCE ❯ **Connection** Have you ever wondered why the sky is blue or the Sun is yellow? When the colorless light from the Sun reaches Earth, it interacts with the atmosphere. The light waves collide with particles in our atmosphere. These particles include molecules of nitrogen, oxygen, argon, water vapor, and pollutants. When light strikes a molecule that is smaller than its wavelength, some of the light is absorbed and then released. Higher frequencies (blues) are absorbed more often than the lower frequencies (reds). These absorbed wavelengths are then radiated out in all directions. The blue wavelengths are scattered throughout the sky. So, when you look up, some of this scattered blue light reaches your eyes.

Why is the sky blue?

Sierra Nevada, CA

Colors of Light What happens to light as it passes through a filter like you used in the Investigation *Concepts of Color?* For example, suppose white light, such as sunlight, shines through a piece of blue glass. The glass absorbs all wavelengths of light except blue. The blue wavelengths pass through the glass to your eyes. If the blue glass is translucent, it still only transmits blue light, but the image is blurry. The color of a transparent or translucent object is the color it transmits.

Color Filters Take a look at the figures below. When white light strikes the shirt, only the wavelengths that you see as blue are reflected. The shirt appears blue under white light. If a color filter is applied to the light and only blue light is shown on the shirt, the blue light is reflected. The shirt still appears to be blue. If another color filter is used, such as red, the red light is absorbed and no light is reflected. This makes the shirt appear black under the red light. The color you see always depends on the color of light that the object reflects.

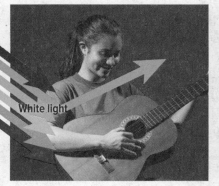
White light

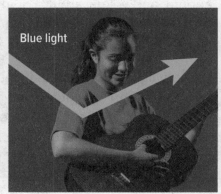
Blue light

Red light

THREE-DIMENSIONAL THINKING

Draw a **model** to **explain** why a white daisy appears blue and the green stem appears black when viewed through a blue filter.

ART Connection Have you ever mixed several colors of watercolor paints to get just the shade you wanted? You know that you can make many different shades from a few basic colors. If you mix too many colors, you get black! Why does that happen?

Pigments Each color of paint in a set of watercolors contains different pigments, or dyes. Each pigment absorbs some colors of light and reflects other colors. Mixing pigments produces many different shades as certain wavelengths are absorbed and fewer colors are reflected to your eyes. As you add each color of pigment, the mixture gets darker and darker because more colors are absorbed. Cyan, magenta, and yellow are the primary pigments. Combining equal amounts of these pigments makes black, as shown in the center of the artist's palette in the figure below on the left.

Light Red, green, and blue are the primary light colors. In the Investigation *Concepts of Color* you shined red, blue, and green light at a piece of white paper. If you shine equal amounts of red light, green light, and blue light at a white screen, each color reflects to your eyes. Where two of the colors overlap, both wavelengths reflect to your eyes and you see a third color. Where the three colors overlap, all colors reflect and you see white light, also shown in the figure below on the right.

Combining Pigments

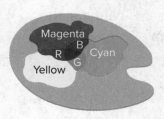

Each primary pigment subtracts color by absorption. Mixing all three pigments equally produces black.

Combining Light

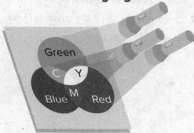

Adding the three primary colors of light produces the colors of the primary pigments and white.

Colors of pigment combine by subtracting wavelengths. Colors of light combine by adding wavelengths.

COLLECT EVIDENCE

How do different colors of light affect how you see color? Record your evidence (B) in the chart at the beginning of the lesson.

A Day in the Life of an Industrial Psychologist

Red makes people think of energy and excitement. That's why it's a popular color for sports cars.

Color psychology is the study of the effect of color on the way people think and behave. For example, the color blue is associated with peacefulness. It tends to make people feel calm. Studies have shown that blue rooms promote creativity.

What words would you use to describe a bright yellow room? Would you say the room is sunny and cheerful? People often connect happiness with yellow and nature with green. Green, like blue, tends to calm people. Hospitals often use green in waiting rooms to reduce people's anxiety. What about orange? Many people connect orange with energy and warmth.

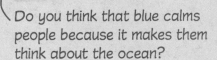

Do you think that blue calms people because it makes them think about the ocean?

Facts about how color affects moods can be fun to learn. However, for some people, it is their business. Industrial psychologists study ways to maximize workers' productivity and safety. Many industrial psychologists pay close attention to the colors used in different areas of the workplace. Those who work in advertising and merchandising choose specific colors for product packages that connect the product inside with certain ideas or emotions.

This waiting room is designed to be soothing.

It's Your Turn

Research and Report Find out more about how a person's culture might influence the way the person perceives colors. Make a poster to share what you learn with your classmates.

Review

Summarize It!

1. **Construct an explanation** on how the model on the right shows that without different wavelengths of light you would not see any colors.

_____

_____

_____

_____

_____

_____

_____

_____

_____

_____

_____

_____

_____

_____

_____

_____

_____

Three-Dimensional Thinking

Use the model below of light entering a raindrop to answer questions 2–4.

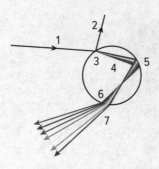

2. What produced the light represented by ray 2?

   A It was absorbed by the drop.

   B It was reflected from the drop.

   C It was refracted by the drop.

   D It was transmitted by the drop.

3. What caused the spread of the colors at point 7?

   A absorption

   B reflection

   C refraction

   D transmission

4. What colors of light make up ray 1?

   A the primary colors of light—red, blue, and green

   B the secondary colors of light—cyan, magenta, and yellow

   C No colors. The ray is black.

   D All of the colors. The ray represents white light.

Real-World Connection

5. Describe how light waves interact with the clothes you are wearing and your eyes.

_____

_____

_____

_____

6. Predict what color a white shirt would appear to be if the light reflected from the shirt passed through a red filter and then a green filter before reaching your eye. Construct a model to support your prediction.

Still have questions?
Go online to check your understanding about colors of light.

REVISIT SCIENCE PROBES

Do you still agree with the statement you chose at the beginning of the lesson? Return to the Science Probe at the beginning of the lesson. Explain why you agree or disagree with that statement now.

EXPLAIN THE PHENOMENON

Revisit your claim on how colors appear from white light. Review the evidence you collected. Explain how your evidence supports your claim.

PLAN AND PRESENT

STEM Module Project
Engineering Challenge

Now that you've learned about the colors of light and how these colors interact, go to your Module Project to develop, make, and test your optical illusion. Keep in mind what happens to light when it is refracted through a prism.

Optical Illusions

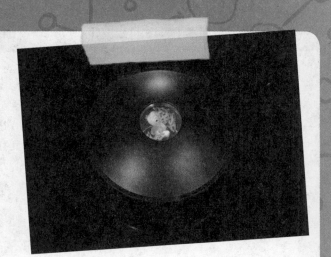

A famous illusionist has hired you to design a new type of optical illusion for a show. How will you do it? To make an optical illusion, you have to use light to make people see an image that is not really there. Here is your challenge:

- You may use only common materials and devices approved by your teacher.

- You must use at least two different interactions of light.

- The image you create must be different from the object(s) in at least two ways (for example, size, orientation, color, or position).

You will then need to develop and use a model to describe how the illusion works as a result of light wave interactions with various materials.

Planning After Lesson 1

Examine the following list of materials that might be used in your optical illusion:

- beaker
- color filters
- prisms
- test tubes
- water
- vegetable oil
- various lenses
- various mirrors
- cardboard box
- plastic box

- clay
- flashlights
- markers
- scissors
- stands
- candles
- matches

To help determine their properties and their possible use in your illusion, classify the materials in the first column based on how they interact with light.

Planning After Lesson 2

Make a graphic organizer with *Reflection* in the center. Around it, show different ideas of how to make this concept the center of an optical illusion.

Planning After Lesson 3

Make a graphic organizer with *Refraction* in the center. Around it, show different ideas of how to make this concept the center of an optical illusion.

Planning After Lesson 4

Brainstorm ideas with others in your group for your illusion using the concepts you have learned. Think about light sources and shadows. How do the various optical devices work, and how could you combine them? Record your ideas.

Use your ideas to design an optical illusion. List the materials and steps you will follow to construct it. Include sketches of your setup. Have your teacher approve your design.

Test Your Illusion

Collect your materials and build your optical illusion. Test your illusion several times. Record your observations in your Science Notebook.

Evaluate Your Illusion

Evaluate the quality and effectiveness of your illusion. Consider these questions:

- Does it meet all the requirements?

- Is your illusion creative and unique?

- How easy is it for an audience to see?

- How different is the image your illusion produces from the object?

Make Revisions

Make a modification to your setup to improve the design. Record your observations and details about your modification. Sketch and label your final setup and note any changes in materials.

Develop Your Model

Develop a model in the space below to show how your illusion functions. In your model, be sure to indicate the following components:

- the type of wave,

- each material and how the light interacts with it,

- the characteristics of the light wave after the interactions,

- the position of the source of the light wave, and

- the path that light travels.

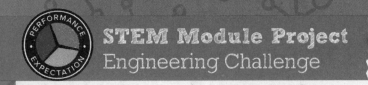
Use Your Model

Demonstrate your illusion for the class. Use your model to help explain the phenomena by writing an explanation of the materials and their properties that allow the illusion to happen.

Based on your work on this project, how could you create a colorful rainbow effect?

Could an astronaut perform this in space? Use your model to help explain your reasoning.

Congratulations! You've completed the Engineering Challenge requirements!

Module Wrap-Up

REVISIT
THE PHENOMENON

Think about everything you have learned in the module about how light acts like a wave. Construct an explanation on where rainbows come from starting with the source and ending with your eye.

INQUIRY

What are one or two questions you still have about the phenomenon?

_____

_____

_____

_____

Choose the question that interests you the most. Plan and conduct an investigation to answer this question.

Information Technologies

ENCOUNTER
THE PHENOMENON

How can you talk to someone when they live across the world?

GO ONLINE
Watch the animation *Sending Signals* to see this phenomenon in action.

Communicate Think about what you know about how signals are shared. With a partner, discuss his or her thoughts. Then record what you both would like to share with the class below.

Out With the Old, In With the New

You work for a cable TV provider, *TV&U*. The company is switching from transmitting signals in an analog format to transmitting them digitally. Many of your customers do not understand the reason for the change. Some think the change will only affect their bills and will not make any difference in quality. Others do not see any benefits to changing to digital in any field.

As a customer-service agent at *TV&U*, you've been asked to explain why digitized signals are more reliable than analog ones. The explanation will be in the form of an insert sent with the customers' monthly bills.

Lesson 1
Communicating with Signals

Lesson 2
Modern Communication with Digital Signals

Start Thinking About It

What do you think of when you hear the word *digital*? Discuss your thoughts with a partner.

STEM Module Project
Planning and Completing the Science Challenge
How will you meet this goal? The concepts you will learn throughout this module will help you plan and complete the Science Challenge. Just follow the prompts at the end of each lesson!

Dots on a Page

A new student joined Antonio's class today. Ms. Brown introduced her and told the class that she was blind. When she sat down next to Antonio she pulled papers out of her bag. The papers were covered with small raised dots instead of print letters. Antonio wondered how this dotted paper worked. This is what he and his classmates said:

Antonio: The dots must represent numbers and the numbers represent letters.

Rafi: The dots represent numbers and letters.

Hama: The dots represent different symbols. Each symbol represents a word.

Who do you most agree with? _____ Explain your thinking about how the dots could represent text.

_____

_____

_____

_____

_____

_____

You will revisit your response to the Science Probe at the end of the lesson.

Communicating with Signals

ENCOUNTER
THE PHENOMENON

| How can you share information?

Can you understand the message in the photo on the left? What about in the space below? Use your understanding of codes to determine what the message says.

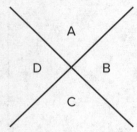 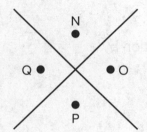

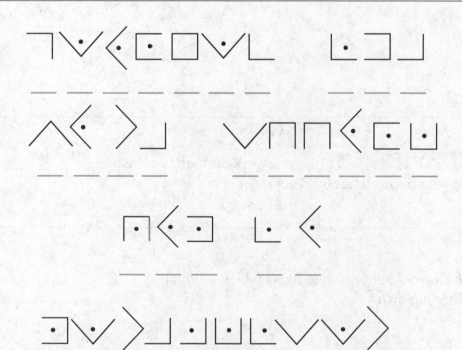

GO ONLINE
Check out *Mystery Message* to see this phenomenon in action.

EXPLAIN
THE PHENOMENON

You may have seen someone using sign language or heard someone speaking another language before. How are they communicating if you cannot understand them? Just like the message in the activity, if you understand the code you can understand what they are communicating. What are some other ways you can share information? Make a claim about how people share information.

CLAIM
You can share information by...

COLLECT EVIDENCE as you work through the lesson.
Then return to these pages to record your evidence.

EVIDENCE

A. What evidence have you discovered to explain how a signal communicates information?

B. What evidence have you discovered to explain how signals are transmitted?

MORE EVIDENCE

C. What evidence have you discovered to explain how "noise" affects signal communication?

When you are finished with the lesson, review your evidence. If necessary, based on the evidence, revise your claim.

REVISED CLAIM

You can share information by...

Finally, explain your reasoning for how and why your evidence supports your claim.

REASONING

The evidence I collected supports my claim because...

What is a signal and how does it communicate?

In the activity you communicated using signals. A **signal** is a piece of information that is communicated through using the senses. Every time you speak you are using sound as a signal to communicate. People who use American Sign Language also use signals to communicate. What is needed for a signal to be understood? Try developing your own signal method to find out!

INVESTIGATION

Signal This

1. With your group, develop a method to send messages using signals. Have each student come up with a message and use the method you created to send each message to the other students in your group. In the space below, record your method and the messages your group sent to each other.

2. Now pair up with another student from a different group. Take turns sending messages to each other. Were you able to interpret your partner's message? Was he or she able to interpret your message? Why or why not?

Sharing Information What do verbal speech, braille, and reading a text all have in common? They are all different types of signals used to send information. The method of how they are sent varies. Vocal cords send information encoded in pressure waves through the air. Reading this text on a page requires a light source to reflect off the page in very specific unique patterns. Your brain interprets this as information encoded in text. Braille encodes information as arrangement of dots, that once felt, can be interpreted. To send a signal the information is encoded. The signal is then sent, or transmitted. A receiver then interprets the signal.

Want more information?
Go online to read more about how signals are used to communicate.

FOLDABLES
Go to the Foldables® library to make a Foldable® that will help you take notes while reading this lesson.

Encoding Signals A signal can be stored, encoded, or transmitted. In the Investigation *Signal This*, you sent messages within your group. Everyone understood the signal because you all agreed what the signal was. When you switched groups it became harder or impossible to understand the message. This happened because you did not understand how the group encoded their signals. To send a signal both the sender and the receiver of the information must both understand how the signal was encoded.

An example of an encoded message happens when hikers leave a signal made from rocks and sticks to inform other hikers of trail dangers or directions. These signals can only be understood if the receiving hiker also understands the signal. Other examples of methods used to encode signals include Morse code and binary. Most devices, like computers, have built-in technology that encodes and decodes information automatically.

COLLECT EVIDENCE

How does understanding signals help you share information? Record your evidence (A) in the chart at the beginning of the lesson.

How can they communicate if they cannot hear the photographer?

How are signals transmitted?

In the previous investigation, your signals were communicated to the people nearby. How could you send a signal to someone far away?

INVESTIGATION

Passing On Signals

1. Sit across the room from your partner. Use the code below to develop a message.

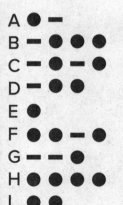
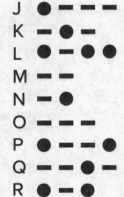

A ● —	J ● — — —	S ● ● ●
B — ● ● ●	K — ● —	T —
C — ● — ●	L ● — ● ●	U ● ● —
D — ● ●	M — —	V ● ● ● —
E ●	N — ●	W ● — —
F ● ● — ●	O — — —	X — ● ● —
G — — ●	P ● — — ●	Y — ● — —
H ● ● ● ●	Q — — ● —	Z — — ● ●
I ● ●	R ● — ●	

2. Record your coded message below.

3. Use a flashlight to send the message to your partner across the room. A dot represents a quick flash of light and a dash represents a longer pause of light.

4. Have your partner send you his or her message. Record this message in the space below.

5. When you are done sending messages, compare notes. Did you understand your partner's message? Record how you could improve the transmission of the messages.

_____

_____

_____

_____

6. What were the benefits of using the flashlight to send the messages?

_____

_____

_____

Transmitting Signals Signals can also be transmitted or passed on. When you talk to another person, you are transmitting information. Signals can be transmitted long distances by using electromagnetic waves such as radio waves, microwaves, or light waves. An advantage to transmitting information with waves is that they do not permanently move matter. They can also be varied in many ways to hold information. One disadvantage of using waves to carry signals is that they lose energy as they travel through mediums. This reduces how far a message can be sent.

Radios, phones, and televisions were developed to send or receive different signals carried by electromagnetic waves or electric signals. Electric signals are encoded in wave pulses and are carried by wires over long distances. Information such as computer data and telephone calls can be converted into electrical signals. The electronic signals for these devices travel at least part of the way through optical fibers. In the next investigation you will discover how optical fibers transmit information.

INVESTIGATION

Fiber Optics

▶ **GO ONLINE** Watch the animation *Fiber Optics* to find out how glass wires are used to transmit signals across distances. Then, complete the graphic organizer below.

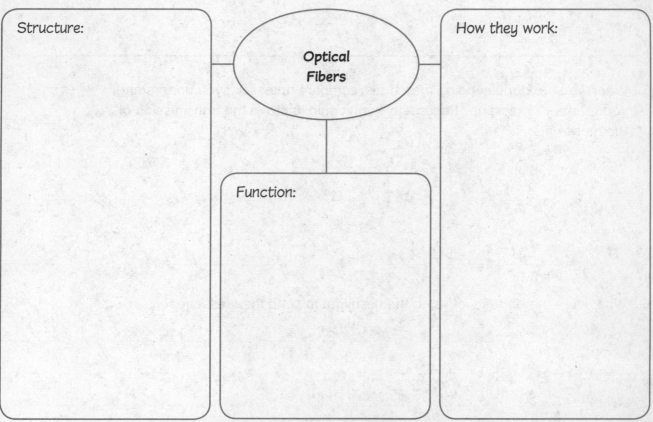

Structure:

Optical Fibers

How they work:

Function:

Electromagnetic Waves As research into electromagnetic waves has progressed, more technologies have used them as a method of communication for a number of reasons. Electromagnetic waves travel very fast (300,000 km/s). Electromagnetic waves allow for fast communication over long distances, such as the video call shown in the figure on the right.

Electromagnetic waves can also be modulated, or modified, to contain information. Wave modulation occurs by changing a property of the wave. Two ways to modulate a wave are to change the wave's amplitude (AM) or the wave's frequency (FM).

THREE-DIMENSIONAL THINKING

WRITING Connection Lighthouses were designed for the function of warning boats of dangerous areas near shorelines. **Construct an argument** for why lighthouses use light instead of sound for sending signals to boats. Cite textual evidence to support your argument.

_____

_____

_____

_____

GO ONLINE for an additional opportunity to explore!

Investigate how electromagnetic waves are used by performing the following activity.

☐ **Explain** how fiber optics are used to communicate across Earth after watching the **Video** *Fiber Optics Communication*.

COLLECT EVIDENCE

How does understanding how signals are transmitted explain how sign language can be used to communicate? Record your evidence (B) in the chart at the beginning of the lesson.

What affects how well a signal is transmitted?

Sometimes when you are talking on a cell phone the signal is crystal clear, and other times you can barely understand the person. What happens to signals as they are transmitted to cause such changes? Let's investigate.

INVESTIGATION

Phone a Friend

1. In a small group of 3–4 students, play the telephone game. Have each person start a message and end the message.

2. Now, play the telephone game in a group of 8–10 students.

3. Finally, play the telephone game with your whole class.

4. Explain what happened to the signal as it was communicated to more and more people.

Signal Noise If you are standing next to your friend and she says something, you will hear her clearly. But what if she said the same thing across a noisy room? You might have to ask her to repeat what she said. Why? The other noises in the room interfered with the sound wave that you were hearing. The same thing can happen in other types of information. A photograph can become too bright when too much light is let into the camera. Microphone feedback happens when electronic signals interfere with each other.

When a signal is transmitted or the information is stored, unwanted and unavoidable modification of the signal will happen. **Noise** is the unwanted modification of a signal. As a wave moves farther away from its source, it can mix with other signals, which causes slight variations in the original signal. You might have noticed this not only in the Investigation *Phone a Friend*, but also in the Investigation *Passing On Signals*. If the receiving person saw someone else's flashlight, his message could have become a part of your message. The source of the noise can be different for each signal, but the information in each of these signals will deteriorate as noise increases.

COLLECT EVIDENCE

How does how well a signal is transmitted affect the information that is sent in the signal? Record your evidence (C) in the chart at the beginning of the lesson.

A Closer Look: Radio Signals

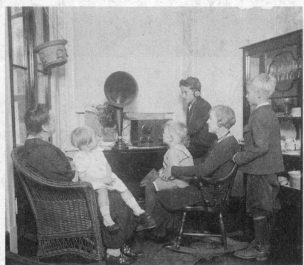

The first radio broadcast was in 1910. Since then radio has continued to be used as a form of communication across the world.

A radio station must do more than simply transmit a wave. It must also send information about the sounds that you are to receive. The sounds produced at the radio station are converted into electric signals. This electric signal is called the signal wave and is used to modify the wave.

The modified carrier wave is converted from an electric signal to a radio wave by using an antenna. The antenna creates an electromagnetic wave that travels outward from the antenna in all directions. The signal from the radio station is strongest close to the broadcasting antenna and becomes weaker as you move away. Eventually, the signal will be too weak to be detected by your radio. This is why radios in New York City do not pick up FM radio stations broadcast in Los Angeles. Bad weather, surrounding mountains, and artificial structures can also interfere with radio transmissions.

It's Your Turn

WRITING **Connection**   Research how television is broadcasted. Create a presentation that shows how signals are sent from a studio to your home.

Summarize It!

1. **Diagram** Create a diagram that shows what happens to a signal as it is transmitted over long distances.

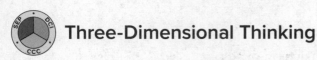

Three-Dimensional Thinking

Examine the model of how light travels through a fiber optic cable.

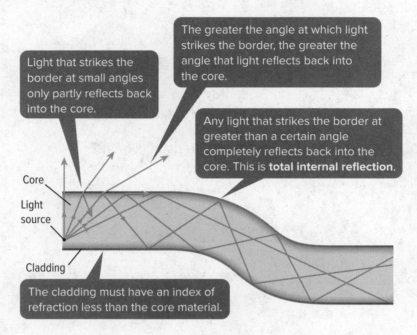

The greater the angle at which light strikes the border, the greater the angle that light reflects back into the core.

Light that strikes the border at small angles only partly reflects back into the core.

Any light that strikes the border at greater than a certain angle completely reflects back into the core. This is **total internal reflection**.

Core

Light source

Cladding

The cladding must have an index of refraction less than the core material.

2. Why does light stay inside an optical fiber?

   A Because of the wave behavior of reflection

   B Because of the wave behavior of refraction

   C Because of the wave behavior of diffraction

   D Because of the wave behavior of transmission

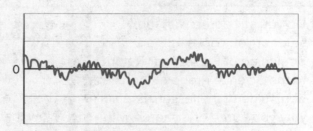

3. The wave shown in the graph above is affected by signal noise. How does this affect the quality of the wave?

   A It increases the quality.

   B It decreases the quality.

   C The quality is not affected by noise.

   D It only affects the wave if you are far away from the source.

Real-World Connection

4. Explain What does it mean to encode a signal? Give an example.

_____

_____

_____

_____

5. Infer Why are electromagnetic waves used to transmit signals?

_____

_____

_____

_____

_____

_____

_____

Still have questions?
Go online to check your understanding about how signals are used to communicate.

REVISIT SCIENCE PROBES

Do you still agree with the student you chose at the beginning of the lesson? Return to the Science Probe at the beginning of the lesson. Explain why you agree or disagree with that student now.

EXPLAIN THE PHENOMENON

Revisit your claim on how you share information. Review the evidence you collected. Explain how your evidence supports your claim.

START PLANNING

STEM Module Project Science Challenge
Now that you've learned about how signals are encoded and transmitted, go to your Module Project to research how television stations transmit signals to your home television. Keep in mind how those signals can travel great distances across the world.

PERFORMANCE EXPECTATION

Spinning Records

A group of friends found a record player that plays music at Opa's grandmother's house. The friends wondered why records are not used as often today. This is what they said:

Opa: I think records are not used as often because records are more expensive to make.

Niran: I think records are not used as often because records can be scratched and the sound would be changed.

Zahara: I think records are not used as often because they only play music and not other sounds.

Ricardo: I think records are not used as often because there is not enough plastic to continue to make them.

Who do you most agree with? _____ Explain your thinking.

_____

_____

_____

_____

_____

You will revisit your response to the Science Probe at the end of the lesson.

Modern Communication with Digital Signals

ENCOUNTER
THE PHENOMENON | Why are tape drives no longer used?

Your teacher will demonstrate how to use an information storage device called a tape drive. Your teacher will place the tape drive into the tape drive player. Record your observations below. Include in your observations the quality of the information. Explain why you might not use one today.

Rewind the Tape!

GO ONLINE
Watch the video *Rewind the Tape!* to see this phenomenon in action.

EXPLAIN
THE PHENOMENON

You have likely heard that most technology is moving away from analog and towards digital technology. You may even use a computer, which uses digital signals, to listen to music or do homework. Many analog devices used to be used for these modern activities. Make a claim about why tape drives are no longer used.

CLAIM

Tape discs are no longer used because...

COLLECT EVIDENCE as you work through the lesson. Then return to these pages to record your evidence.

EVIDENCE

A. What evidence have you discovered to explain how analog signals transmit information?

B. What evidence have you discovered to explain how digital signals transmit information?

MORE EVIDENCE

C. What evidence have you discovered to explain how digital information advances science?

When you are finished with the lesson, review your evidence. If necessary, based on the evidence, revise your claim.

REVISED CLAIM

Tape discs are no longer used because...

Finally, explain your reasoning for how and why your evidence supports your claim.

REASONING

The evidence I collected supports my claim because...

What is an analog signal?

Film cameras are a type of tape drive. Tape drives are made of a continuous piece of tape wound on a spool. When the tape is pulled through a device, the device translates the information on the tape. How is this an analog system? Let's find out!

LAB Continuous Signals

Safety

Materials

alcohol thermometer	water
600-mL beaker	stopwatch
hot plate	ring stand
1-hole stopper	clamp

Procedure

1. Read and complete a lab safety form.

2. Fit an alcohol thermometer into the 1-hole stopper.

   CAUTION: *Do not force the thermometer or it could break.*

3. Fill the beaker with 400 mL of water.

4. Place the beaker on a hot plate. Use the ring stand and a clamp to hold the base of the thermometer above the bottom of the beaker.

5. Turn on the hot plate and begin warming the water to 50°C.

6. In the table on the right, fill in how long the thermometer was at each temperature in seconds.

7. Follow your teacher's instructions for proper cleanup.

Temperature (°C)	Time at temperature (s)
25	
30	
35	
40	
45	
50	

Analyze and Conclude

8. Plot the temperature and time data you collected on the grid below. Plot temperature on the vertical axis and time on the horizontal axis. Label the axes and add a title to your plot. Draw a line that goes through the most points.

9. On average, how long did the temperature reading stay at a specific value?

_____

_____

_____

10. An alcohol thermometer is an analog thermometer. What do you think analog means?

_____

_____

_____

Analog Signals In the Lab *Continuous Signals* the thermometer gave a continuously changing temperature reading. Analog signals change continuously over time. For instance, think about an analog clock. The hands continuously move over the face of the clock. If the small hand has moved two segments of time, it means that twice as much time has passed than if only one segment of time has passed. Both the clock and the thermometer are representations of something. The clock represents time and the thermometer represents temperature. These devices are representations, or analogies, of the ideas they are representing. **Analog signals** are a representation of the information that is communicated. Until the introduction of computers, almost all instruments used for measuring were analog.

Notice that the analog signal in the figure to the right is a continuous smooth curve. Analog signals can be a range of values. Recall that radio signals are a type of signal that are transmitted. Radio signals are analog signals. The towers that send music to your radio at home send these signals through electromagnetic waves. The waves of a radio tower are a continuous signal that is translated by your home radio into sound waves.

Analog Signal

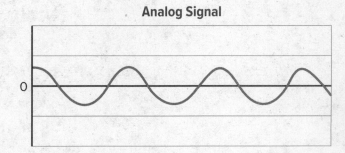

0

THREE-DIMENSIONAL THINKING

A speedometer in a car is designed to tell you how fast the car is moving at all times. **Construct an explanation** about what the information represents.

_____

_____

_____

_____

_____

_____

What happens to an analog signal over time?

An analog signal is continuous over time. How would information be recorded or stored in an analog signal? Let's investigate!

 Want more information?
Go online to read more about modern communication with digital signals.

INVESTIGATION

Without a Trace

Below is a continuous color pattern.

1. In your Science Notebook, trace the image below as precisely as possible with colored pencils. Try to ensure all the information about the image is contained.

2. Once you have completed your trace of the image, trade Science Notebooks with a partner. Take a piece of paper, and trace your partner's rendition of the above image. Again, try to ensure all the information about his or her image is contained.

3. Compare your trace of your partner's image to the original above. What do you notice about the quality of your trace?

_____

_____

_____

Analog Noise in the Investigation *Without a Trace*, did you notice the quality of the information in the image declined? Recall that noise is an unavoidable modification of a signal. When an analog signal is recorded, the noise is recorded along with the original signal. Over time, noise accumulates and the information deteriorates. Think about a time that your home radio did not sound clear. The noise that the radio made is the result of noise accumulating on the original signal. The radio is translating the signal correctly, but the signal has changed the original information due to noise. This is why a tape drive sounds less clear than the music from a computer or portable media player. The noise in the signal has deteriorated the information stored on the tape drive over time.

Scientists have developed ways to filter noise out of analog signals. However, when this is done the original signal is still altered. When the original signal is altered, the information contained in the signal becomes altered. This can result in a loss of quality from the original information.

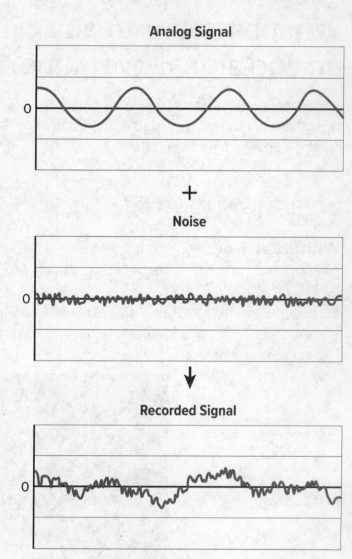

Analog Signal

+

Noise

↓

Recorded Signal

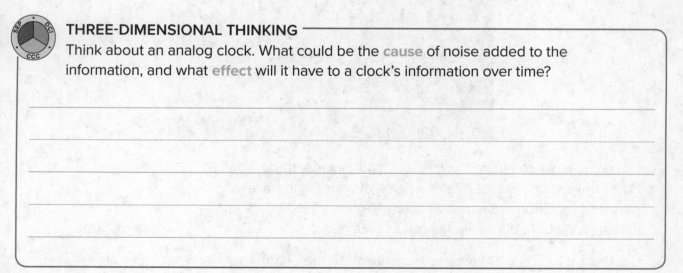

THREE-DIMENSIONAL THINKING

Think about an analog clock. What could be the cause of noise added to the information, and what effect will it have to a clock's information over time?

_____

_____

_____

_____

_____

COLLECT EVIDENCE

How does the way analog signals transmit information support your claim about why tape drives are no longer used? Record your evidence (A) in the chart at the beginning of the lesson.

What is a digital signal?

You likely do not use a tape drive to listen to music. Today's society is moving toward a digital means of playing and listening to music. What does it mean to say that something is digital? Let's investigate!

 Information Stairs

Safety

Materials

digital thermometer	water
600-mL beaker	stopwatch
hot plate	ring stand
1-hole stopper	clamp

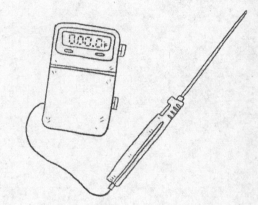

Procedure

1. Read and complete a lab safety form.

2. Fit a digital thermometer into the 1-hole stopper.

3. Fill the beaker with 400 mL of water.

4. Place the beaker on a hot plate. Use the ring stand and a clamp to hold the base of the thermometer above the bottom of the beaker.

5. Turn on the hot plate and begin warming the water to 50°C.

6. In the table below, fill in how long the thermometer was at each temperature in seconds.

Temperature (°C)	Time at temperature (s)
25	
30	
35	
40	
45	
50	

7. Follow your teacher's instructions for proper cleanup.

Analyze and Conclude

8. Plot the temperature and time data you collected on the grid below. Plot temperature on the vertical axis and time on the horizontal axis. Label the axes and add a title to your plot. Draw a line that connects each point.

9. What happened between the values that you measured?

_____

_____

_____

10. How is this thermometer different than the alcohol thermometer?

_____

_____

_____

Digital Signals The digital thermometer displays discrete values. Each value has a specific amount and is not continuous. Examine the digital clock in the image to the right. The time is 9:27. The clock only changes when the time is 9:28. This is discrete information about the time of day. Your digital thermometer gives discrete values for the temperature until the next value. Digital information is not continuous.

A **digital signal** is an electric signal whose value changes between two values. A digital signal is not continuously changing values like analog signals. The information being communicated is converted into numbers or digits to be displayed, transmitted through wave pulses, or stored. Information such as computer data and telephone calls can be encoded into electrical signals. A signal to or from a computer is encoded into **binary numbers,** such as the two values—on (1) and off (0).

Digital Signal

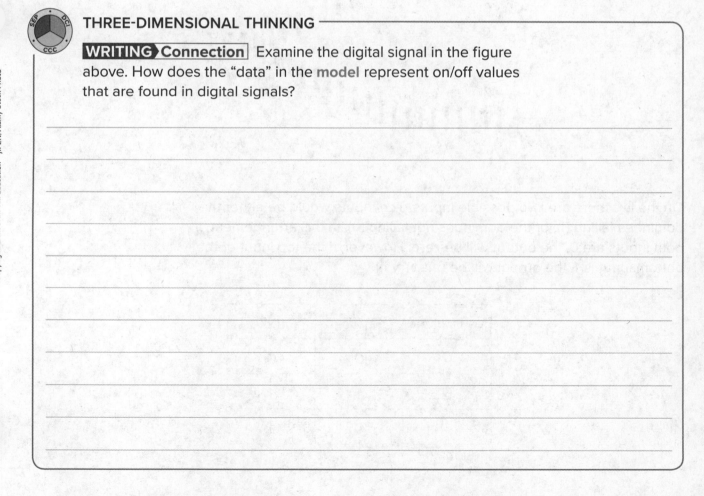

THREE-DIMENSIONAL THINKING

WRITING Connection Examine the digital signal in the figure above. How does the "data" in the model represent on/off values that are found in digital signals?

_____

_____

_____

_____

_____

_____

_____

_____

_____

_____

How does a digital signal encode information?

Digital signals are only composed of two possible values. If you were only given two possible values, how could you encode information in a signal? Let's investigate!

INVESTIGATION

The Computer Domino Effect

A computer has many different functions, but all of the computer's abilities are a result of inputs and outputs. An input is information that the computer receives. An output is the computer's translation of the input information. To make a simple model of this system, obtain some dominoes from your teacher.

1. Analyze the domino layout below, and arrange your dominoes similarly.

On the left there are two possible inputs. The inputs would be either the dominoes falling (1), or the dominoes not falling (0). In this arrangement, if both inputs are 0, the output will be zero. However, if the top input or the bottom input is 1, the output will be one. Try it!

input	input	output
0	0	0
0	1	1
1	0	1

2. What would the output have been if you knocked down both inputs?

_____

_____

This process outputs a 1 if either or both inputs are 1. For other processes, a computer may need to have an output of 1 if either input is a 1, but not both. Look at the domino layout below.

3. Arrange your dominoes as shown below.

4. Input the values that have an output of 1 and complete the table below.

input	input	output
0	0	
0	1	
1	0	
1	1	

5. If you received an output of 1, what do you know about the inputs?

_____

_____

01110011 01000011
01101001 01100101
01101110 01100011
01100101

Suppose you only want the output to be 1 if both inputs are 1. Look at the domino layout below. In this setup, to have an output that is not 0 both inputs must be 1.

6. Arrange your dominoes as shown below.

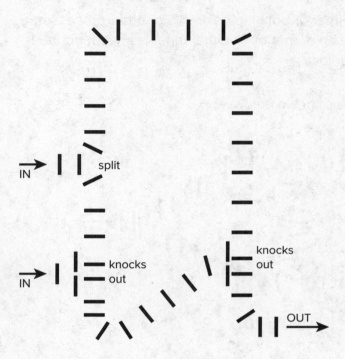

7. Input the values that have an output of 1, and complete the table below.

input	input	output
0	0	
0	1	
1	0	
1	1	

8. Why is the long domino layout at the top of the figure useful in making this process work?

_____

_____

_____

To write a number larger than 1 in binary, a digit is placed to the left, as in the decimal system. After the digit is larger than 1, the binary digit returns to 0 and a 1 is then placed to the left. For example, two becomes 10. The decimal three is represented as 11. The decimal four then is 100, and so on. Say you want your dominoes to be an adding machine. With two inputs you can add combinations of 0s and 1s together. The outputs represent the sum of the input digits in binary.

9. Arrange your dominoes as shown below.

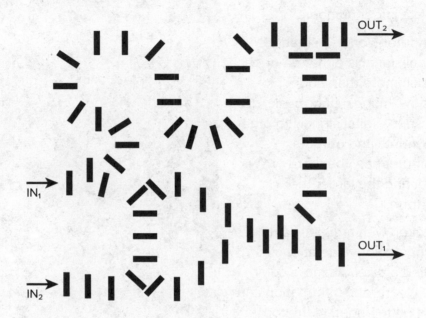

10. Choose two values to add together and add them using the domino computer. Complete the table below.

Input 1	Input 2	Output 2	Output 1
0	0		
0	1		
1	0		
1	1		

11. How does the domino computer translate digital information?

_____

_____

_____

Binary Information Information, such as computer data and telephone calls, can be encoded into electrical signals. A signal to or from a computer is encoded into binary numbers. Recall that a computer can translate information that is represented by 1s and 0s which represent on/off. In the Investigation *The Computer Domino Effect* the domino computer is designed to take any combination of 1s and 0s and do simple addition. If the domino computer had more inputs and outputs, it could calculate larger numbers.

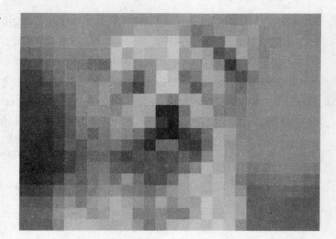

This is how a real computer works. Instead of dominoes, the electrical signal is either on or off. Computers can do much more than add numbers. They can show images, play music, do homework, and even send digital signals to other computers. The more inputs and outputs technology like a computer has, the more information it can hold, and the larger the calculations it can perform.

Think about a photo taken with a digital camera. A digital photo holds one color value at one particular location called a pixel. As more color values are added, the clearer the information can be. Look at the photos on the right. In the top image, the digital information exists, but it is not enough to make out what the image actually looks like. As more information is added, the photo becomes clearer.

For digital sensors and probes, information is continually reaching the sensor. Think about a digital camera. Light is continuously reaching the camera, but each pixel can hold only one value or color. The camera records each pixel in a process called sampling. For most digital cameras, the camera takes a sample of each pixel 1×10^7 times per second. This is why a video from a digital camera looks continuous. Sampling is used in all digital probes. If you had a digital thermometer in the Lab *Information Stairs* that had a high sampling rate, the data would look similar to the analog information.

COLLECT EVIDENCE

How does the way digital signals transmit information support your claim about why tape drives are no longer used? Record your evidence (B) in the chart at the beginning of the lesson.

What happens to a digital signal over time?

Digital signals are sent in discrete units. To store or copy the information, the copy only includes two values. What would happen to the information over time?

Trace Back

Below is a color pattern of two possible colors.

1. In your Science Notebook, trace the image below as precisely as possible with colored pencils. Try to ensure all the information about the image is contained.

2. Once you have completed your trace of the image, trade Science Notebooks with a partner. Take a piece of paper, and trace your partner's copy of the image. Again, try to ensure all the information about his or her image is contained.

3. Compare your trace of your partner's image to the original above. What do you notice about the quality of your trace?

_____

_____

_____

Digital Noise Just like analog signals, when digital signals are sent, noise is added to the original signal. Examine the figure to the right. When noise is added to a digital signal, the information can still be clear to the receiver. In the Investigation *Trace Back,* you likely had a few areas that were not an exact trace of the original image. If you received this trace, but knew that red and blue were the only colors coming from the original, it would be easy to interpret what the original image looked like.

A device that receives and translates a digital signal is only expecting one of the two values, on or off. Noise then is easily filtered off without significant deterioration to the original information even when transmitted over long distances. Higher quality information can be received when the original information is not altered by the noise added to the signal. This makes digitized signals a more reliable way to encode and transmit information than analog signals.

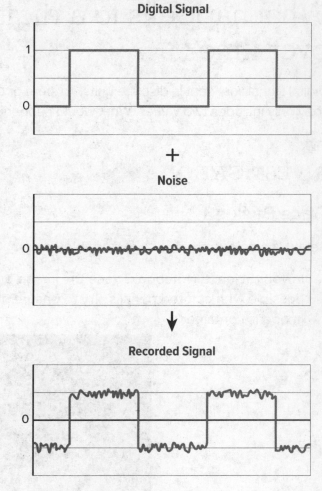

Digital Signal

Noise

Recorded Signal

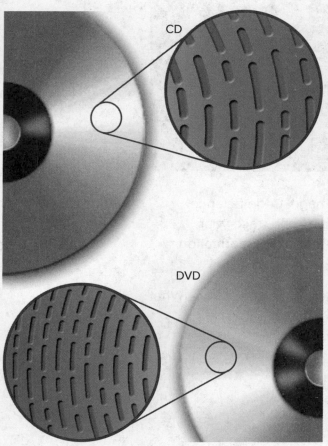

CD

DVD

Digital Storage When you save music to your home computer, the computer saves the song as digital information. Then when you decide to play the song, the computer recalls the digital information the same way every time. Look at the figure to the left. Every time the CD or DVD is played, the information is the same. The pits do not degrade, so the information remains and is unchanged.

Because of this ability, digital signals are easy to store without the worry of degradation of the information over time. To retrieve information stored in digital form, the device that recalls the information must be able to translate a digital signal. Recall that information must be translated by the receiver for information to be interpreted. This is why you cannot place a DVD into a CD player. The CD player is not designed to decode the information on a DVD.

How does digital technology advance science and science investigations?

Digital signals are more resistant to noise, and can hold large amounts of information. In what ways are scientists using digital technology to advance science?

Read a Scientific Text

As technology has improved, space telescopes have to be updated to obtain and transmit more information. This advance in technology extends our ability to explore, measure, and model the universe.

CLOSE READING

Inspect

Read the passage *Amazing Miniaturized 'SIDECAR' Drives Webb Telescope's Signal.*

Find Evidence

Reread the passage. Determine the central ideas or conclusions of the text. Underline what evidence shows that an upgrade to a digital signal will help provide scientists with better information.

Make Connections

Communicate With your partner, discuss if this evidence would be enough to convince you that digital signals are more reliable in transmitting information.

PRIMARY SOURCE

Amazing Miniaturized 'SIDECAR' Drives Webb Telescope's Signal

Many technologies have become so advanced that they've been miniaturized to take up less space and weigh less. That's what happened to some electronics being built for the James Webb Space Telescope that will convert analog signals to digital signals and provide better images of objects in space when they're sent to scientists on Earth. The James Webb Space Telescope is being built by Northrop Grumman.

The electronic components on the Webb telescope are called "SIDECAR ASIC." SIDECAR ASIC means "System for Image Digitization, Enhancement, Control And Retrieval Application Specific Integrated Circuit". The SIDECAR has been miniaturized from a volume of about one cubic meter (35.3 cubic feet) down to a small circuit that fits in your hand.

To understand what the SIDECAR will do, it's similar to what is happening to broadcast television signals when they changed from broadcasting analog signals to digital signals in February 2009. Like televisions, the Webb telescope is getting several of those "converter boxes." One benefit digital signals have over analog signals is that digital signals can be easily transmitted and stored.

SIDECAR is a tiny advanced low-noise, low-power microprocessor-based control chip that was designed by Teledyne Imaging Sensors, Thousand Oaks, Calif. It's about the size of a half-dollar and can do the same job as an electronics box weighing 20 pounds. Its smaller weight also makes it easier to launch. As the acronym implies, the SIDECAR sits next to the detector like a sidecar on a motorcycle.

Source: National Aeronautics and Space Administration

Digital Probes Space telescopes are not the only place that digital information is useful. Digital thermometers, like the one you used in the Lab *Information Stairs*, are used by scientists to measure accurate data about temperature. The thermometer measures electrical resistance in a wire, which is related to the temperature of that wire. The thermometer calculates the temperature based on the resistance, and displays a discrete value.

Almost all probes and scientific measurements today are done with digital technology. Digital audio recordings help scientists understand what is happening beneath the ocean. Digital sensors are used in particle accelerators to understand what is happening at the smallest levels of matter. Digital signals sent by the Mars rovers told scientists about the planet's composition. The advancement of digital technology leads to further advancement of science. Each probe is designed to serve a particular function.

THREE-DIMENSIONAL THINKING

Sara is using an analog clock and a meterstick to measure the speed that a ball rolls for her lab. **Design a solution** to improve her mean standard deviation using digital technology.

_____

_____

_____

_____

_____

COLLECT EVIDENCE

How does the way that digital information advances science support your claim about why tape drives are no longer used? Record your evidence (C) in the chart at the beginning of the lesson.

A Day in the Life of a Marine Biologist

Just as a GPS can provide information about the location of a car, satellite tracking technology can track wild animals. One group of biologists who use satellite tracking technology is marine biologists. Marine biologists attach digital tracking devices to aquatic life, which helps in understanding the oceans. Data from the tracking technology provides scientists with information about the animals' locations, migrations, and populations.

Marine biologists use digital tracking methods to study marine populations. Marine life, from sharks near southern California to seals north of Alaska, have suffered a population decrease over the past several decades. Scientists have discovered that overfishing, changing environments, and many other factors cause population declines in marine life. Information collected from satellite tracking is useful in determining ways to protect animals in the ocean and ways to help restore the populations. Without digital tracking technology, scientists would not be able to collect valuable information about these ecosystems.

It's Your Turn

READING Connection What are some other factors contributing to decreasing populations beneath the waves? What can you do? Choose a marine species and develop an action plan to help stabilize their habitat. Share the action plan with your class.

Review

Summarize It!

1. **Compare and contrast** analog and digital signals. Be sure to include the information a signal contains and the method of sending information.

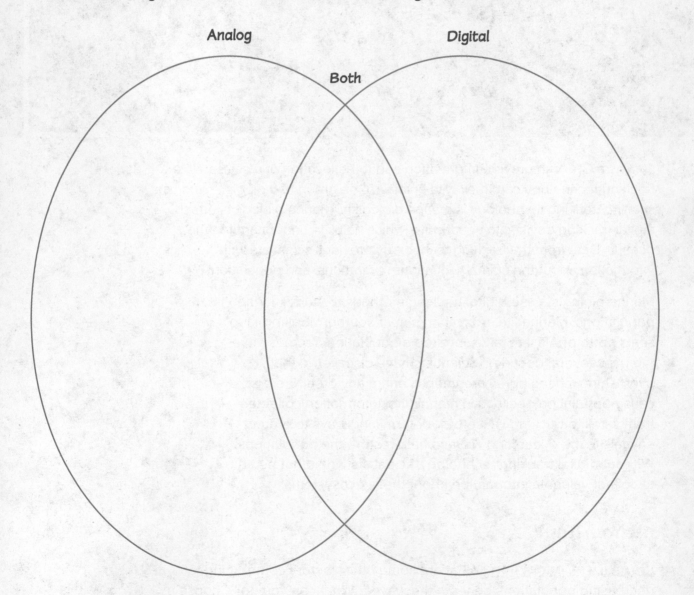

Analog

Digital

Both

Three-Dimensional Thinking

Kris works with a rover that sends her data about the surface of a distant planet. The digital information is translated by her computer and provides data that she can use for her studies.

2. Which model best describes the signal that Kris' computer receives?

A

Analog Signal

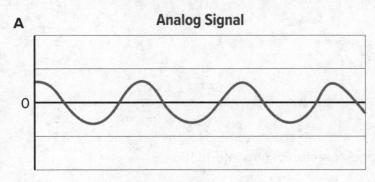

B

Digital Signal

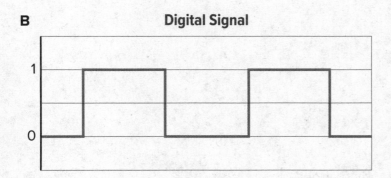

C

Noise

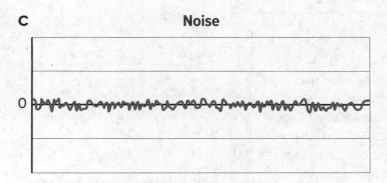

D

Recorded Signal

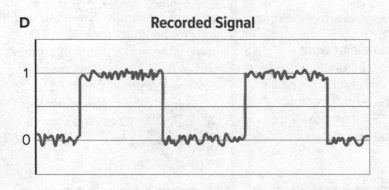

Real-World Connection

3. **Argue** You and a friend are playing with portable two way radios. Your friend says this is the best form of digital communication she knows. Create an argument about why the toys are not digital communication.

_____

_____

_____

_____

_____

4. **Explain** Create an explanation for why a home computer is designed to use a binary number system for storing and communicating information.

_____

_____

_____

_____

_____

 Still have questions?
Go online to check your understanding about modern communication with digital signals.

REVISIT
 **SCIENCE PROBES**
Do you still agree with the student you chose at the beginning of the lesson? Return to the Science Probe at the beginning of the lesson. Explain why you agree or disagree with that student now.

EXPLAIN
THE PHENOMENON

Revisit your claim what makes digital signals more reliable than analog signals. Review the evidence you collected. Explain how your evidence supports your claim.

PLAN AND PRESENT
STEM Module Project
Science Challenge

Now that you've learned about communicating with digital signals, go to your Module Project to use your research to complete a table comparing and contrasting analog and digital signals. Keep in mind how these signals can help you watch live video from across the world.

PERFORMANCE · EXPECTATION

Out With the Old, In With the New

You work for a cable TV provider, *TV&U*. The company is switching from transmitting signals in an analog format to transmitting them digitally. Many of your customers do not understand the reason for the change. Some think the change will only affect their bills, and will not make any difference in quality. Others do not see any benefits to changing to digital in any field.

As a customer-service agent at *TV&U,* you've been asked to explain why digitized signals are more reliable than analog ones. The explanation will be in the form of an insert sent with the customers' monthly bills.

Planning After Lesson 1

Begin your research on how data is transmitted by television companies. Organize your findings in the space below. Be sure to draw from a variety of different sources of information, including texts, graphical, video, and digital, and cite your sources.

Planning After Lesson 2

Compare and contrast each type of data and how they
are recorded and stored.

Analog	Digital

Compare and contrast each type of data and how they are transmitted and
interpreted.

Analog	Digital

Plan Your Presentation

Use the space below to sketch a plan of your insert.

Construct Your Presentation

Construct your insert. Be sure to integrate information to support the claim that digitized signals are more reliable than analog signals for encoding and transmitting information. The insert should include media or a visual display to help clarify the scientific explanation. Keep your audience in mind as you write. Many of the customers reading the paragraph may not be familiar with science terms and concepts.

Share Your Presentation

Share the insert that you developed with others. Examine and evaluate several of the inserts developed by your classmates.

Give feedback on an insert. Some questions to keep in mind during your feedback include:

- Which features best helped support the claim?
- How does the insert reach the audience?
- How does the media or visual display support or clarify the claim?
- What improvements would you make to your insert?

Congratulations! You've completed the Science Challenge requirements!

Module Wrap-Up

REVISIT
THE PHENOMENON

Think about everything you have learned in the module about communication with analog and digital signals. Construct an explanation why you can view a live show across the world.

INQUIRY

What are one or two questions you still have about the phenomenon?

_____

_____

_____

_____

Choose the question that interests you the most. Plan and conduct an investigation to answer this question.

Glossary

Pronunciation Key

Use the following key to help you sound out words in the glossary.

a	back (BAK)		Ew	food (FEWD)
ay	day (DAY)		yoo	pure (PYOOR)
ah	father (FAH thur)		yew	few (FYEW)
ow	flower (FLOW ur)		uh	comma (CAH muh)
ar	car (CAR)		u (+ con)	rub (RUB)
E	less (LES)		sh	shelf (SHELF)
ee	leaf (LEEF)		ch	nature (NAY chur)
ih	trip (TRIHP)		g	gift (GIHFT)
i (i + com + e)	idea (i DEE uh)		J	gem (JEM)
oh	go (GOH)		ing	sing (SING)
aw	soft (SAWFT)		zh	vision (VIH zhun)
or	orbit (OR buht)		k	cake (KAYK)
oy	coin (COYN)		s	seed, cent (SEED)
oo	foot (FOOT)		z	zone, raise (ZOHN)

English — A — Español

absorption/convex lens   **absorción/lente convexo**

absorption: the transfer of energy from a wave to the medium through which it travels.

amplitude: the maximum extent of the repeating quantity from equilibrium.

analog signal: a representation of the information that is communicated.

absorción: transferencia de energía desde una onda hacia el medio a través del cual viaja.

amplitud: distancia entre el punto más alejado de una onda y el punto de equilibrio.

señal analógica: representación continua de un tipo de información.

B

binary numbers: encoded signal with two values to or from a computer.

sistema binário: señal codificada con dos cifras que es usada en ordenadores y sistemas electrónicos.

C

concave lens: a lens that is thicker at the edges than in the middle.

concave mirror: a mirror that curves inward.

convex lens: a lens that is thicker in the middle than at the edges.

lente cóncavo: lente que es más grueso en los extremos que en el centro.

espejo cóncavo: espejo que dobla hacia adentro.

lente convexo: lente que es más grueso en el centro que en los extremos.

convex mirror: a mirror that curves outward.

espejo convexo: espejo que curva hacia afuera.

D

diffuse reflection: reflection of light from a rough surface.

digital signal: an electric signal whose values change between two values.

reflexión difusa: reflexión de la luz en una superficie rugosa.

señal digital: señal eléctrica que tiene cifras que cambian entre dos valores.

F

focal point: the point where light rays parallel to the optical axis converge after being reflected by a mirror or refracted by a lens.

frequency: the number of times the pattern repeats in a given amount of time.

punto focal: punto donde rayos de luz paralelos al eje óptico convergen después de ser reflejados por un espejo o refractados por un lente.

frecuencia: cantidad de vezes que se repite un modelo en una cantidad de tiempo.

I

intensity: the amount of energy that passes through a square meter of space in one second.

intensidad: cantidad de energía que atraviesa un metro cuadrado de espacio en un segundo.

L

law of reflection: law that states that when a wave is reflected from a surface, the angle of reflection is equal to the angle of incidence.

lens: a transparent object with at least one curved side that causes light to change direction.

light: electromagnetic radiation that you can see.

longitudinal (lahn juh TEWD nul) wave: a wave in which the disturbance is parallel to the direction the wave travels.

loudness: how you perceive the energy of a sound wave.

ley de la reflexión: ley que establece que cuando una onda se refleja desde una superficie, el ángulo de reflexión es igual al ángulo de incidencia.

lente: objeto transparente que tiene, al menos, un lado curvo que hace que la luz cambie de dirección.

luz: radiación electromagnética que puede verse.

onda longitudinal: onda en la que la perturbación es paralela a la dirección en que viaja la onda.

volumen: percepción de la energía de una onda sonora.

M

mechanical wave: a wave that can travel only through matter.

medium: a material in which a wave travels.

onda mecánica: onda que puede viajar sólo a través de la materia.

medio: material en el cual viaja una onda.

N

noise: the unwanted modification of a signal.

ruido: modificación no deseada de un señal.

O

opaque: a material through which light does not pass.

opaco: material por el que no pasa la luz.

P

pitch: the perception of how high or low a sound is; related to the frequency of a sound wave.

tono: percepción de qué tan alto o bajo es el sonido; relacionado con la frecuencia de la onda sonora.

R

radiant energy: energy carried by an electromagnetic wave.

energía radiante: energía que transporta una onda electromagnética.

real image: an image that forms where rays converge.

reflection: the bouncing of a wave off a surface.

refraction: the change in direction of a wave as it changes speed in moving from one medium to another.

regular reflection: reflection of light from a smooth, shiny surface.

imagen real: imagen que se forma donde los rayos convergen.

reflexión: rebote de una onda desde una superficie.

refracción: cambio en la dirección de una onda a medida que cambia de velocidad al moverse de un medio a otro.

reflexión especular: reflexión de la luz desde una superficie lisa y brillante.

S

signal: a piece of information that is communicated through using the senses.

sound wave: a longitudinal wave that can travel only through matter.

señal: pieza de información que es comunicada por los sentidos.

onda sonora: onda longitudinal que sólo viaja a través de la materia.

T

translucent: a material that allows most of the light that strikes it to pass through, but through which objects appear blurry.

transmission: the passage of light through a medium.

transparent: a material that allows almost all of the light striking it to pass through, and through which objects can be seen clearly.

transverse wave: a wave in which the disturbance is perpendicular to the direction the wave travels.

translúcido: material que permite el paso de la mayor cantidad de luz que lo toca, pero a través del cual los objetos se ven borrosos.

transmisión: pasaje de una onda a través de un medio.

transparente: material que permite el paso de la mayor cantidad de luz que lo toca, y a través del cual los objetos pueden verse con nitidez.

onda transversal: onda en la que la perturbación es perpendicular a la dirección en que viaja la onda.

V

virtual image: an image of an object that your brain perceives to be in a place where the object is not.

imagen virtual: imagen de un objeto que tu cerebro percibe que está en un sitio donde no está el objeto.

W

wave: a disturbance that transfers energy from one place to another without transferring matter.

wavelength: the distance between one point on a wave and the nearest point just like it.

onda: perturbación que transfiere energía de un lugar a otro sin transferir materia.

longitud de onda: distancia entre un punto de una onda y el punto más cercano similar al primero.

Index

Italic numbers = illustration/photo
Bold numbers = vocabulary term
lab = indicates entry is used in a lab
inv = indicates entry is used in an investigation
smp = indicates entry is used in a STEM Module Project
enc = indicates entry is used in an Encounter the Phenomenon
scc = indicates entry is used in a STEM Career Connection

Index